Supporting Change in Autism Services

Supporting Change in Autism Services explores the theoretical and practical dimensions of improving service provision for children, young people and adults with autism. The core aim of the book is to identify and critically examine some of the key factors that either facilitate or inhibit the implementation of good autism practice at both practitioner level and workplace level. It shows practitioners and students how to successfully translate autism theory into practice across service contexts and showcases a range of practitioner case studies throughout the text in order to illustrate effective implementation.

Topics explored include:

- controversies and ambiguities in autism policy, theory and discourse;
- understanding autism in an inclusive context;
- enabling participation;
- making sense of behaviour;
- autism and interprofessionalism;
- strategic planning for autism friendly services;
- bridging the implementation gap.

This book is essential reading for anyone interested in improving services for people with autism in the education, social care, health and voluntary sectors.

Jackie Ravet is a Senior Lecturer and Director of the Autism & Learning Masters Programme at the University of Aberdeen, UK.

Supporting Change in Autism Services

Bridging the gap between theory and practice

Jackie Ravet

Routledge
Taylor & Francis Group

LONDON AND NEW YORK

First published 2015
by Routledge
2 Park Square, Milton Park, Abingdon, Oxon OX14 4RN

and by Routledge
711 Third Avenue, New York, NY 10017

Routledge is an imprint of the Taylor & Francis Group, an informa business

British Library Cataloguing in Publication Data
A catalogue record for this book is available from the British Library

Library of Congress Cataloging in Publication Data
Ravet, Jackie.
Supporting change in autism services : bridging the gap between theory and practice / Jackie Ravet.
pages cm
1. Children with autism spectrum disorders--Education. I. Title.
LC4717.R38 2015
371.9--dc23
2014033647

ISBN: 978-0-415-50827-8 (hbk)
ISBN: 978-0-415-50828-5 (pbk)
ISBN: 978-0-203-12567-0 (ebk)

Typeset in Sabon
by Saxon Graphics Ltd, Derby

Printed and bound in Great Britain by
TJ International Ltd, Padstow, Cornwall

To my family, my students and to E.M. for teaching me so much about autism.

Contents

Acknowledgements

Many people have no idea that they influenced the writing of this book.

First and foremost my thanks must go to all the pupils with autism whom I have had the privilege to teach. I would not be in any position to write a book like this if it were not for the fascinating learning journeys we shared together. These pupils were my best (and sometimes harshest!) critics, and taught me what it really means to live with autism. Much of what I have learnt from them has been poured into this book. I will never forget any of them.

I also wish to thank the many postgraduate students who have attended my autism courses and contributed so generously to discussions about autism, inclusion and professional practice. Their reflections and insights have helped to shape my own professional learning and have deeply enriched my understanding of autism. I have drawn on this on every page and hope that future students will benefit from it.

A very special thank you must go to former students Mike Culley, Paula Jacobs and Gillian Ronald who kindly allowed me to use their work as a basis for the case studies in chapters 3, 4 and 6.[1] Their examples of good practice bring theory to life and will inspire others to go further, and dig deeper, to provide the best possible support for clients with autism.

I must also thank Meg Taylor for reading a draft of the book and for contributing so much, over many years, to the thinking that underpins it.

Finally, I am most grateful to Sarah Tuckwell and Alison Foyle at Routledge for their unswerving faith in the value of this book. Thank you for your patience, understanding and encouragement.

I draw on several of my published research papers in various chapters of this book.

The following are reprinted and adapted with the kind permission of Taylor & Francis Ltd, www.tandfonline.com:

Inclusive/exclusive? Contradictory perspectives on autism and inclusion: the case for an integrative position, *International Journal of Inclusive Education* (2011), 15/6, 667–682.

From interprofessional education to interprofessional practice: exploring the implementation gap, *Professional Development in Education* (2012), 38/1, 49–64.

The following is reprinted and adapted with the kind permission of the British Institute of Learning Disabilities (BILD), www.bild.org.uk:

Interprofessional training in autism: impact on professional development and workplace practice, *Good Autism Practice* (2011), 12/1 79–87.

Note

1 All names and identifiers used in the case studies have been changed to ensure anonymity and confidentiality.

Introduction

Many years ago, after I was appointed as a Support for Learning teacher in a secondary school, I was quietly informed that I would be responsible for all the learners with autism in the support base and mainstream classrooms. Though I knew nothing about autism at that time, and had never taught this group of children before, I approached the challenge with missionary zeal. I considered myself a competent teacher, having emerged fairly recently from a four-year BEd degree. My head was still full of educational theory, my shelves were stocked with the latest books, and I had recent experience, in the same school, of working with a range of youngsters with what were then referred to as 'special educational needs'. I therefore assumed that I was well equipped for what lay ahead and felt ready to step up to my new responsibilities.

On my first day I met Graham. He was a tall, pale, nervous-looking boy who refused to sit down near me, his peers, or, indeed, at all during our entire first encounter. He stood facing the wall with his coat firmly zipped up to his chin and his hands covering his ears for much of the lesson. He refused to turn around. The other children nonchalantly accepted this and informed me, in reassuring tones: 'Never mind Graham, Miss, that's just how he is.' This was followed by the perplexing warning: '...but don't tell him off or he might start head-banging.' Neither a gentle nor a firm approach, nor any manner of enticements could persuade Graham to interact with me. Worryingly, several of them induced the threat of head-banging accompanied by loud noises.

I was shocked. I had never met a pupil like Graham. In a single lesson I exhausted my entire toolkit of ideas for engaging with him. He did not take part in any of the activities the other children completed, and he did not say a single word to anyone. Even his body language was impenetrable; there was no sense of what he might be thinking or, more importantly, feeling, though it was quite clear that he would not, or could not, join in. My sense of failure was utterly complete. This boy had learnt nothing, and so it continued over several nerve-racking sessions. It would have been easy to conclude that Graham's 'problems' were to blame, and that I should simply expect very little of him.

Thankfully I was forced to come to a different conclusion. Though all the young people on the autism spectrum I met during these early days were very different from Graham, and from each other, my overwhelming feeling was that I was not fit to teach any of them. I did not understand what made these children tick, and it was obvious that all my training, experience, even my instincts, could not help me. I was very soon knocking on the Headteacher's door begging to be sent on the next autism-training course. Fortunately, it came quickly and had an immediate impact. I experienced so many 'eureka' moments during my first, intensive, three-day training, that I was barely the same teacher by the end of it. I couldn't wait to get back to the classroom.

What helped me so much was the detailed explanation of the condition, which enabled me to grasp the underlying meaning of the children's unique behaviour. An insight into the key pedagogical principles for supporting them was utterly invaluable. After this, and many other training courses, I slowly began to make better sense of Graham's signals, and found effective ways of making contact with him and including him in lessons alongside other children. I came to know how to avoid head-banging. To my great relief, I began to be able to teach Graham. And he began to learn.

This difficult introduction to autism taught me a salutary lesson that is at once obvious but profound, though still not widely appreciated. It taught me that, instead of rejecting certain individuals as 'challenging', or assuming that their difficulties are fixed and inevitable, it is important that professionals recognise the decisive role that their own limitations play in the teaching and learning context. I learnt that the problem was me, not Graham, and that it was to do with my teaching, not with autism. This insight came as a revelation to me, for it meant that the possibility of changing things were, to a great extent, in my own hands. I could do something about it and this was hugely empowering. It completely turned my thinking about teaching and learning with this group of children upside down.

Now, years later, I am the director of postgraduate courses in autism in a university context, and I repeatedly hear variations of the story above from my own students, whether they be teachers or social care workers, therapists or employment support officers. They are attending these courses for the very same reasons that first drove me to my Headteacher's door; they worry that they may be failing individuals with autism and they want to learn how to improve their practice so that it is more effective and inclusive.

This book is written for professionals in this predicament and for anyone interested in improving services for people with autism in the education, social care, health and voluntary sectors. The book's broad purpose is to explore the theoretical and practical dimensions of improving autism provision. However, its core aim is to identify and critically examine some of the key factors that either facilitate or inhibit the implementation of good autism practice at both practitioner level and workplace level. We therefore start at the individual practitioner level to analyse the various influences, positive and negative, that currently mediate professional development in autism. We then look beyond the individual practitioner to consider the power of interprofessional and collaborative working to determine how good autism practice can be disseminated more widely and, crucially, more effectively, in order to maximise the benefits to clients with autism.

In order to address this aim, the book critically analyses a range of theoretical perspectives within the autism literature and critically explores current autism research and evidence-based practices. It also showcases a selection of case studies, which provide 'lived' examples of the implementation process. The importance and value of this focus will be self-evident to professionals working with this client group. Most professionals are deeply concerned about the quality of the service they offer, and need knowledge, understanding, skills and resources to help them to improve. This has certainly provided an important motive for writing this book. However, the problem with autism provision across public services runs far deeper than this, so it is important that the current gap between policy and implementation is recognised and understood within the wider sociocultural, legislative and policy context. There have been many changes within these contexts in recent years, inextricably linked to a growing public awareness of autism and the steep rise in the numbers of people diagnosed with the condition. They are also linked to acknowledgement of the widespread social, educational and economic exclusion associated with this vulnerable group, brought to light by individuals with autism, their families, support groups, charities, researchers and professionals in the field. Let us look at this more closely.

What is the problem with autism services?

> The main issue I want to get across is getting the support. If I could get help…from professionals with an understanding of autism and Asperger Syndrome, I feel I would move forward at a much faster rate.
>
> (Adult with autism: Daly 2008, p. 6)

It is important to stress that there have been many positive changes in the lives of individuals with autism over the past 50 years (Bancroft et al. 2012). There are more services, there is more support, greater understanding and considerably more acceptance of the condition compared to the past. The lives of many are full of possibility and hope. Yet, there is still a long way to go.

The poor quality of service provision for children, young people and adults with autism across the United Kingdom is now a major concern and is a key driver of recent national autism strategies. This concern is linked to two important factors. Firstly, it is associated with the rising incidence of the condition, which is currently estimated at around 1:100 (Baird et al. 2006, Brugha et al. 2009). This incidence rate is far higher than previous estimations and clearly has significant consequences for service planning and provision, plus high cost implications for the state (Knapp et al. 2010). Crucially, it means that growing numbers of practitioners across public services are regularly required to include and support individuals with autism in their everyday practice. Secondly, concern is linked to a widespread consensus that the educational and social needs of this group are generally complex, highly individual in nature and difficult to identify (Jones et al. 2008). This is exacerbated by a lack of knowledge and understanding of autism amongst frontline professionals, which limits their capacity to address these needs effectively (Daly 2008, Rosenblatt 2008, Bancroft et al. 2012). It has therefore been widely concluded that poor training is a key barrier to the effective inclusion of individuals with autism.

For example, in the education sector in the UK, a 'presumption of mainstreaming' resulting from the introduction of anti-discrimination and inclusion legislation (DfES 2001, DDA 2005, EA 2010, SEED 2004) has meant that many more teachers and allied professionals are now being called upon to teach learners with autism in mainstream classrooms. Many of these pupils would, formerly, have been educated in special schools or units. It is very difficult to gauge how many children and young people with autism are now educated in mainstream, as, until recently, statistics of this sort had never been widely or systematically collected. However, based on 2011 census figures, it is currently estimated that there are 700,000 people with autism in the UK and around 137,607 children with autism between the ages of 4–16 (NAS 2014). An estimated 121,012 children with autism in this age bracket reside in England. Around two-thirds of them are currently educated in mainstream classrooms in England (DfE 2010). This means that the vast majority of teachers will be called upon to teach students with autism at some point in their careers.

In response to this rise in numbers, there have been repeated attempts to audit educational provision for learners with autism in order to identify gaps and plan for the future (HMIE 2006, Jones et al. 2008). All of these studies have highlighted patchy standards and significant training issues. For example, two National Autistic Society (NAS) reports (Batten & Daly 2006, Batten et al. 2006) found that 65% of parents in Scotland, England and Wales were dissatisfied with the level of understanding of autism amongst teachers in their child's school, and associated this with low attainment and poor educational progress. Likewise, the HMIE report (2006) acknowledged that 'the majority of teachers and non-teaching staff in mainstream schools (in Scotland) did not have a sufficiently good working knowledge of autism' (p. 25). Studies of teacher perceptions indicate that they largely agree with these findings. Teachers acknowledge that there are problems for pupils with autism, and, importantly, complications for themselves and other pupils when they lack sufficient awareness of the condition and its implications for learning (Robertson et al. 2003, Jones et al. 2008). Furthermore, research into the perceptions of pupils with autism provides valuable insights into the specific difficulties they encounter when taught in environments that are not adapted to their needs, and by teachers who do not understand their unique learning style (Molloy & Vasil 2004, Humphreys & Lewis 2008).

The most damaging outcomes for the pupils themselves are stress and unhappiness, persistent underachievement and high rates of school exclusion. Though exclusion figures for specific groups of pupils are difficult to establish, one large-scale survey of 1300 respondents found that one in five (21%) pupils with autism had been excluded from school, and that 67% of these had been excluded more than once (Reid & Batten 2007). These are troubling statistics that far exceed exclusion levels for other groups of children (Humphrey & Lewis 2008). Research therefore confirms the urgency of training in autism for education staff and related professionals so that they might meet the needs of learners with autism more effectively, and carry out their legal duties in line with inclusion policy and legislation.

Over the past decade, reviews of provision for clients with autism across Health and Social Care services have identified comparable service gaps and inequalities (PHIS 2001, NIASA 2003, Batten et al. 2006, Scottish Executive 2006, Rosenblatt 2008, Bancroft et al. 2012). For example, a recent Scottish Government report (2008) acknowledged that the 'way local services are structured and organised discriminates against (people with autism)', resulting in their 'near exclusion from services' (p. 3). Rosenblatt (2008) identified gaps in diagnostic services, and reports that just under half of the primary care trusts in England have no autism-specific diagnostic provision at all. She also reports that in a study of 1412 adults with autism, 60% indicated that they had experienced problems getting support from their local authority or health authority, and that 42% of this group were told that this was because there were no appropriate services available. More recently, Bancroft et al. (2012) reported that 55% of those who responded to a UK-wide autism survey complained that diagnosis took 'too long' and was 'too stressful' (p. 9).

Daly (2008) found that Community Health Partnerships across Scotland face comparable problems to those in England and emphasised the need for more training for health professionals. GPs are highlighted as the group in greatest need of professional development in autism. This possibly explains why just under 30% of adults in a survey of 175 adults with autism in Scotland rated their GP's understanding of autism as 'bad' or 'very bad' (ibid). There is evidence that people with autism are at greater risk of health and mental health problems linked to poor support and service provision (Daly 2008, Rosenblatt 2008). Homelessness, unemployment and dependence on benefits are also prevalent amongst adults with autism (ibid.). For example, only 15% of adults with autism are in full-time employment (Bancroft et al. 2012) and 59% 'don't believe or don't know if they will ever get a job' (ibid. p. 27).

Years ago, the Public Health Institute of Scotland (PHIS) Report (2001) recognised that poor training amongst service practitioners was the common denominator underpinning unacceptable levels of social, academic and economic exclusion amongst clients with autism. The Scottish Executive responded by funding a two-year research study into professional training needs. The subsequent report (MacKay & Dunlop 2004) noted the paucity of training, the widespread fragmentation of training provision, and also the lack of 'a strategic plan' for autism training (p. 51). A small body of evidence suggests that some progress has been made as a result of increased training provision in subsequent years. For example, there are indications of improvements in attitudes amongst mainstream teachers, increased levels of confidence amongst parents, and enhanced knowledge amongst medical staff in some areas (SIGN 2007). Despite this, sizeable training gaps still remain, resulting in a lack of knowledge, skills and expertise amongst large numbers of professionals working across statutory services (ibid.). Individuals with autism pay a heavy price for these gaps. However, in a report of the economic costs of autism, the National Audit Office (NAO 2009) reminds us that everyone bears the cost when unmet needs lead to dependence on the state and ongoing crisis intervention. It is estimated that autism costs the UK economy £28.2 billion a year (ibid.).

A significant consensus has therefore evolved over the last decade concerning the need for enhanced professional training in autism to address longstanding and wide-ranging inequalities. Unfortunately, years of anti-discrimination and inclusion legislation, specifically targeted at marginalised groups, has not succeeded in preventing this accumulation of disadvantage. The reasons for this should give pause for thought and deserve closer analysis. (A detailed discussion of this issue features in chapter 2.) However, the result has been the introduction of the first ever disability-specific legislation in England and Northern Ireland. This has taken the form of an Autism Act (England 2009, Northern Ireland 2011), which covers provision in a range of areas including health, social care, employment and training. The Act contains two important provisions: the requirement for the development of a national autism strategy, and the requirement for statutory guidance for local authorities and local health bodies on supporting the needs of individuals with autism. In Scotland and Wales there are national autism strategies with a similar focus, but without legislation (Welsh Assembly Government 2008, Scottish Government 2011).

In order to explore, and critically analyse, the factors that enable and inhibit change across services for clients with autism, we will first set the scene by exploring what autism is and examining autism in an inclusive context. Chapter 1 therefore explores perceptions of autism, the manifestations of the condition, the diagnostic criteria and the key theories of autism. However, we pay particular attention to the complexities, controversies and ambiguities relating to autism theory and research and how they influence and, frequently, undermine service provision. Note, therefore, that this section has a narrow focus on the essentials of the condition and a critique of key theories. It will not linger on, nor elaborate, discussion of historical perspectives, the diagnostic process or details of biological processes and scientific brain research. There are many other books on the market that cover this terrain more squarely and fully, and their numbers continue to grow rapidly (e.g. Roth 2010).

In chapter 2 we turn our attention to inclusion – the key policy framework for service provision – and the impact of this on practitioners and clients. The focus is on the conflicting discourses on inclusion that influence practice and the dilemmas these create for practitioners supporting clients with autism. Here, it is argued that practitioners require a clear theoretical grasp of autism and its relationship to inclusion theory if they are to have a chance of proceeding to effective implementation.

The remaining four chapters then explore what actually happens when practitioners attempt to put theory into practice in the workplace, and analyse the barriers to implementation they encounter. This exploration is illustrated with practitioner enquiries into their own autism practice.

Thus, in chapter 3 we critically examine some of the autism-specific strategies used across service settings, which enable clients with autism to participate and learn. Here, the term 'learning' is used in its broadest sense, and does not refer only to learning at school. So, it is about how individuals with autism can be supported to learn to live independently, socialise, access employment, maintain health, etc. – as well as learn in an academic sense. Links are made to current literature and research with regard to assessment, target-setting and person-centred planning, strategies and their evidence base. A case study is provided to exemplify how some of these strategies can be put into practice.

Chapter 4 is about making sense of the behaviour of individuals with autism, as this can be highly problematic for professionals who do not understand the condition. This chapter first deals with the thorny issue of how so called 'challenging' behaviour might be defined, especially in contexts informed by an inclusive philosophy and ethos. A variety of strategies to prevent, avoid and replace challenging and self-destructuve behaviours is explored in detail. Functional analysis, risk assessment and crisis intervention are also discussed. A case study taken from a classroom context will illuminate how one practitioner grapples with the underlying meaning of 'challenging' behaviour and attempts to address it.

Interprofessionalism is the central theme of chapter 5 because of the priority it is given in current policy and legislation, its powerful links to inclusion theory and autism research, and the important role it plays in the lives of people with autism. This chapter therefore discusses what interprofessionalism is, why it matters and how it is achieved. It also looks critically at the implementation of policy and theory through the eyes of students who attempt to enhance their interprofessional practice by engaging with a wide range of partners. The case study highlights their perceptions of the benefits of interprofessionalism for their own practice, for colleagues, for workplace provision and for clients with autism. The study also illuminates the barriers to interprofessionalism encountered by the students and explores their impact on service outcomes.

Chapter 6 explores the concept of the 'autism friendly workplace'. This concept is important as it is hailed, within the literature, as the ultimate aim of service improvement, and is held up as a worthy aspiration for all those working with clients with autism. However, the autism friendly workplace can only be attained by ongoing workplace monitoring and auditing to establish the quality of practice and provision. This cannot be achieved via an ad-hoc, laissez-faire approach but necessitates coordinated, holistic planning for training and practice improvement. The purpose of this chapter is therefore to explore this auditing and planning process in detail and to bring the main arguments in the theoretical sections of the book to a conclusion by showing how all the key themes – inclusion, autism awareness, approaches and interventions, behaviour support and interprofessionalism – lie at the heart of strategic planning for autism friendly services. The chapter then goes on to explore how strategic planning might be approached via a structured and collaborative process of auditing and target-setting. A case study within a residential setting provides an example of how one practitioner applies this strategic planning process to implement a small-scale improvement at workplace level.

In the final chapter, chapter 7, we reflect upon key issues relating to the transformation of theory into practice, and consider their impact on the process of supporting change in the workplace. The factors that facilitate and inhibit good autism practice will be identified in order to illuminate the workings of the 'implementation gap' across service provision. The implications of these factors for practitioners, for training providers and for service managers will be analysed, as well as the wider implications for national planning for autism in the UK and beyond.

Here it will be emphasised that though autism training is vital for the development of autism awareness and an understanding of inclusion, training alone cannot bridge the implementation gap. Indeed, if we are to maximise the impact of training, practitioners and service managers have a responsibility to address the various barriers to implementation that arise, again and again, in different service environments. Though these vary in their particulars across contexts, they are commonly associated with the culture of the workplace, leadership, and attitudes to autism and inclusion. They are also linked to service organisation and traditional ways of conducting service practice and delivery.

It should be clear, then, that this is not a general 'what is autism?' textbook. Rather, the book aims to shine a light on professional action and impact and the factors that confound them. The focus on action – what practitioners actually do to bring about change – is especially relevant in the context of the Autism Act (England 2009, Northern Ireland 2011) and the national autism strategies in Scotland (Scottish Government 2011) and Wales (Welsh Assembly Government 2008). These initiatives demand that services widen access and improve the quality of provision for clients with autism. So there is much to do. The focus on 'impact' is crucial in the current climate of concern for effectiveness and best value within a challenging economic milieu. I therefore hope that, by the end of this book, readers will have grasped the complex interplay of factors that require consideration before effective action and successful impact can be achieved.

References

Autism Act (2009) London: The Stationery Office. Accessible: http://www.legislation. gov.uk/ukpga/2009/15/pdfs/ukpga_20090015_en.pdf (accessed July 2014).

Autism Act (Northern Ireland) (2011) London: The Stationery Office.

Baird, G., Simonoff, E., Pickles, A., Chandler, S., Loucas, T., Meldrum, D. & Charman, T. (2006) Prevalence of disorders of the autism spectrum in a population cohort of children in South Thames: the Special Needs and Autism Project (SNAP), *Lancet*, 368, 210–215.

Bancroft, K., Batten, A., Lambert, S. & Madders, T. (2012) *The Way We Are: Autism in 2012*, London: National Autistic Society.

Batten, A., Corbett, C., Rosenblatt, M., Withers, L.T. & Yuille, R. (2006) *Make School Make Sense – Autism & Education: The Reality for Families Today*, London: National Autistic Society.

Batten, A. & Daly, J. (2006) *Make School Make Sense: Autism and Education in Scotland – The Reality for Families*, London: National Autistic Society. Accessible: bera.ac.uk/publications (accessed May 2008).

Brugha, T., McManus, S., Meltzer, H., Smith, J., Scott, F.J., Purdon, S., Harris, J. & Bankart, J. (2009) *Autism Spectrum Disorders in Adults Living in Households throughout England: Report from the Adult Psychiatric Morbidity Survey 2007*, Leeds: NHS. Accessible: www.ic.nhs.uk/asdpsychiatricmorbidity07 (accessed Sept. 2009).

Daly, J. (2008) *I Exist: The Message from Adults with Autism in Scotland*, Glasgow: National Autistic Society (Scotland).

Department for Education (DfE) (2010) *Special Educational Needs in England, January 2010: Statistical First Release*, London: DfE.

Department for Education and Skills (DfES) (2001) *Inclusive Schooling*, London: DfES.

DDA (Disability Discrimination Act) (2005) London: The Stationery Office. Accessible: http://www.legislation.gov.uk/ukpga/2005/13/contents (accessed July 2014).

EA (Equality Act) (2010) London: The Stationery Office. Accessible: http://www. legislation.gov.uk/ukpga/2010/15/contents (accessed July 2014).

HMIE (2006) *Education for Pupils with Autism Spectrum Disorders*, Livingston: HMIE.

Humphreys, N. & Lewis, S. (2008) 'Make Me Normal': The views and experiences of pupils on the autistic spectrum in mainstream secondary schools, *Autism*, 12, 23–46.

Jones, G., English, A., Guldberg, K., Jordan, R., Richardson, P. & Waltz, M. (2008) *Educational Provision for Children & Young People on the Autism Spectrum Living in England: A Review of Current Practice, Issues and Challenges*, London: Autism Education Trust. Accessible: www.autismeducationtrust.org. uk (accessed Nov. 2008).

Keen, D. & Ward, S. (2004) Autistic Spectrum Disorder: A child population profile, *Autism*, 8, 39–48.

Knapp, M., Romeo, R. & Beecham, J. (2009) Economic cost of autism in the UK, *Autism*, 13, 317–336.

MacKay, T.A.W.N. & Dunlop, A.W.A. (2004) *The Development of a National Training Framework for Autistic Spectrum Disorders: A Study of Training for Professionals Working in the Field of ASD in Scotland*, London: National Autistic Society.

Molloy, H. & Vasil, L. (2004) *Asperger Syndrome, Adolescence & Identity*, London: Jessica Kingsley.

National Audit Office (2009) *Supporting People with Autism Through Adulthood*, London: The Stationery Office.

National Autistic Society (NAS) (2014): Statistics. Accessible: http://www.autism.org.uk/about-autism/myths-facts-and-statistics/statistics-how-many-people-have-autism-spectrum-disorders.aspx (accessed July 2014).

NIASA (National Initiative for Autism: Screening & Assessment) (2003) *National Autism Plan for Children*, London: National Autistic Society.

PHIS (Public Health Institute of Scotland) (2001) *Autistic Spectrum Disorders Needs Assessment Report*, Glasgow: NHS.

Ravet, J. & Taylor, M. (2010) Interprofessional development in autism: Effectiveness, impact and implications for training & service providers. Accessible: www.abdn.ac.uk/education/programmes/autism.shtml (accessed Aug. 2010).

Reid, B. & Batten, A. (2007) *Make School Make Sense for Me: Children & Young People with Autism Speak Out*, London: National Autistic Society.

Robertson, K., Chamberlain, B. & Kasari, C. (2003) General education teachers' relationship with included students with autism, *Journal of Autism & Developmental Disorders*, 33, 123–130.

Rosenblatt, M. (2008) *I Exist: The Messages from Adults with Autism in England*, London: National Autistic Society.

Roth, I. (2010) *The Autism Spectrum in the 21st Century*, London: Jessica Kingsley.

Scottish Executive (2006) *Autistic Spectrum Disorder Needs Assessment Report (2001): Scottish Executive Report on Implementation and Next Steps*, Edinburgh: Scottish Executive.

Scottish Government (2011) *The Scottish Strategy for Autism*, Edinburgh: Scottish Government.

SEED (Scottish Executive Education Department) (2004) Education (Support for Learning) (Scotland) Act, Edinburgh: SEED.

Scottish Government (2008) *Commissioning Services for People on the Autism Spectrum: Policy and Practice Guidance*, Edinburgh: Scottish Government. Accessible: www.scotland.gov.uk (accessed April 2009).

Scottish Government (2011) *The Scottish Strategy for Autism: Overview*, Edinburgh: Scottish Government.

SIGN (Scottish Intercollegiate Guidelines Network) (2007) *Assessment, Diagnosis and Clinical Interventions for Children and Young People with Autism Spectrum Disorders: A National Clinical Approach*, NHS Scotland. Accessible: www.sign.ac.uk (accessed March 2009).

Welsh Assembly Government (2008) *Autism Spectrum Disorder Strategic Action Plan for Wales*, Cardiff: Welsh Assembly Government.

Chapter 1

Autism

Controversies and ambiguities

In order to set the context for this book, it makes sense to begin by exploring the nature of autism and the main theories that claim to explain it. In doing so, the many controversies and ambiguities associated with the condition, which can create confusion for practitioners, will be highlighted and explored. This discussion will help to explain why good autism practice can be difficult to implement.

However, before we start we must decide what to call the condition throughout this book and how to refer to those with a diagnosis. This is important because words are powerful. Whether we are aware of it or not, our words betray our attitudes and beliefs about autism, and thus have an influence on others and, crucially, on the autism community. It therefore matters very much how we label the condition and those who live with it.

The vast majority of books currently on the market refer to 'autism spectrum disorder' and to those with the condition as 'autistic'. It might be argued that use of the term 'disorder' discriminates negatively against people with autism as it emphasises dysfunctionality and occludes strengths (Baron-Cohen 2000). Similarly, it might be argued that to label people 'autistic ' is highly disrespectful since it suggests that their entire being and identity cannot be disassociated from their medical condition.

By contrast, throughout this book, and in a growing number of more recent publications, you will notice use of the terms 'autism spectrum condition' and 'people with autism'. These terms are used to avoid negative language. The word 'condition' is, arguably, more value neutral than the word 'disorder', but at the same time it does not obscure the existence of a medical category or deny the reality of those with a diagnosis. Likewise, using the phrase 'people with autism' rather than 'autistic people' avoids the assumed association between autism, being and identity.[1]

There has been much debate about the value and impact of these new terms and others like them (Roth 2010), but there is currently no consensus as to which terms best apply. The debate will, doubtless, rage on for a time, until a critical mass of publications are using the new terminology and the old negative labels slip into disuse. It is important to be in the vanguard of this transition, given its profound implications for individuals with a diagnosis, and for research and practice in the field. The issue of labelling is explored in greater detail in chapter 2.

Autism spectrum condition: what is it?

This section must begin with a note of caution since we still do not know, with any certainty, what autism is or what causes the condition. However, this is not to imply that we have not learnt a great deal about autism since 1943 when the severe and complex form of autism was first identified and delineated by Leo Kanner, an American paediatrician, and 1944 when the more subtle, high-functioning form of autism was first investigated and named by Hans Asperger, an Austrian Psychiatrist (see box 1.1). The point is that much of what we allegedly 'know' has continually been challenged, refined or revised ever since, with direct implications for perceptions of the condition, the forms of support we provide and the interventions we design.

Box 1.1: Early descriptions of autism

Leo Kanner

Kanner was an American psychiatrist who wrote 'Autistic Disturbance of Affective Contact' (1943), based on a five-year study of eleven children whom he described as 'odd' and as having an 'inability to relate themselves in an ordinary way to people and situations from the beginning of life'.

Kanner produced a nine-point scale of the nuclear features of the condition:

- Inability to develop relationships
- Delay in acquisition of language
- Non-communicative use of spoken language
- Delayed echolalia
- Pronominal reversal
- Repetitive, stereotyped play
- Maintenance of sameness
- Good rote memory
- Normal physical appearance

Hans Asperger

Asperger was a Viennese paediatrician who wrote 'Autistic Psychopathies in Childhood' (1944, translated by Wing 1981), in which he described a number of boys who found it difficult to 'fit in' despite a seemingly good level of ability and fluent speech. The boys had significant difficulties with:

- Social language interaction
- Repetitive steroetypical behaviours
- Intense fixations
- Limited understanding of gesture and facial expression
- Poor motor co-ordination

There is clear overlap between Kanner's and Asperger's observations. They both borrowed the term 'autism' from psychiatrist Eugen Bleuler, who first used it in 1911 to describe the social withdrawal associated with schizophrenia. Literally translated, the word autism means 'selfism'.

After the publication of Kanner's work, many other researchers began to develop point-counting systems for the identification of autism (e.g. Rutter et al. 1971, Gillberg & Gillberg 1989).

For example, from the 1940s right through to the 1970s, there was considerable support for the theory that autism was a psychogenic disorder caused by poor parenting and associated, in particular, with a cold, unloving 'refrigerator mother' (Bettelheim 1967). However, research accumulating in the field of neurology during the 1960s and 1970s, particularly that associated with the early work of Rimland (1964), gradually overshadowed and superseded this theory, though not before it caused considerable harm to a large number of families. By contrast, the latest research posits that autism is essentially a neurodevelopmental disorder, i.e. a disorder of the developing mind and brain caused by a genetic anomaly that is somehow activated by an environmental trigger as yet unidentified (Lathe 2006). There is speculation that the trigger, or triggers, might be linked to trauma during pregnancy or birth, infection, hormonal influences, or to a range of pollutants, such as heavy metals in water or toxic chemicals in food. However, as yet, no clear consensus has emerged on the matter. The idea that the MMR vaccine is a key trigger has now been largely rejected (Gerber & Offit 2012), though some parents continue to insist upon a link (Hilton et al. 2007). Whatever the nature of the trigger, it is speculated that this genetic pre-disposition and environmental trigger somehow 'act on the susceptible brain to produce ASD [sic]' (Lathe 2006, p. 211). It is these brain changes that are thought to alter the developmental pathway of the child with autism and account for the behavioural manifestations of the condition discussed below.

Though the precise mechanism that underpins this causal sequence is still far from understood, autism 'is now firmly established as a disorder of the developing mind and brain' (Frith 2003, p. viii). Indeed, brain research utilising new scanning technologies has lent considerable weight and legitimacy to this claim (Boucher 2009). Much of the brain research emerging in this area focuses on the unusually large size of the brain in very young children but the lack of brain growth in middle childhood and thereafter (Courchesne et al. 2011). Atypical connectivity also seems to be characteristic of the autistic brain (Courchesne 2004, Courchesne & Pierce 2005). Neural changes within the following areas have been noted by several different researchers:

- **Prefrontal cortex** – responsible for social perception, planning and strategising
- **Cerebellum** – linked to motor control and associative learning
- **Limbic system** – associated with memory, emotion generation and recognition
- **Corpus callosum** – responsible for information sharing across the two hemispheres

(Just et al. 2007, Sokolowski & Corbin 2012, Allely et al. 2013, Broek et al. 2014 and Edmonson et al. 2014)

It is not within the limits of this book to explore this research in any detail. However, what is interesting about the findings above are the apparent correlations between the areas of the brain that appear to have undergone neural changes, and those responsible for the various functions that operate differently in individuals with autism. Researchers therefore posit a causal connection between the two (Muller 2007).

Yet, fascinating and exciting though this research is, it is still in its infancy and raises many questions (Boucher 2009). For example, it already seems clear from the research that disconnectivity in autism does not follow a particular and consistent pattern but takes various forms with various effects on different neural circuits within the growing brain – some impacting on communication, some on memory, others on emotions, and so on (ibid.). It is uncertain how these different forms arise and whether they are related or entirely discrete in terms of their etiology (ibid.). If they are discrete, this suggests that the characteristics they impact upon are independent of each other. If so, why do they appear to be related when expressed in everyday behaviour (ibid.)?

Disconnectivity theory does not, therefore, provide a comprehensive explanation of all of the characteristics of autism and its various forms. However, it provides another tantalising piece of the autism puzzle. A key difficulty for practitioners lies in making sense of, and evaluating, the validity of this highly technical and specialised medical research, and understanding how it should inform our perceptions of the condition. Keeping up with the fast pace of change within the field is also an ongoing challenge.

To complicate matters further, we must remind ourselves that the understanding of autism explored within the British and European research literature is highly 'situated' in a socio-cultural sense, as well as temporally. Thus, though the manifestations of autism will be the same in any context, the understanding of the condition that prevails in Asian or African cultures may be very different to that which prevails in white European cultures because of the divergent underlying values and beliefs that shape them (Taylor Dyches et al. 2004).

For example, in a small-scale study of beliefs relating to autism and causation amongst Asian and white British families, autism was largely understood to be caused by biomedical factors like genetics or birth trauma amongst the European parents, whereas it was largely attributed a divine or magical providence, like God's will or punishment, amongst Asian parents (Mockett et al. 2009). Thus, autism is by no means a unitary phenomenon but is subject to multiple interpretations.

Even within the UK autism research community, definitions and theories advanced by different researchers may vary in their detail, depending on researcher values and beliefs and the particular discipline from which their theories emerge. This adds yet another layer of interpretation and complexity to the issue. Years ago, Williams (1997) summed up the changing concept of autism and her words still hold true today:

> Over the years 'autism' has been considered a form of spiritual possession, a mental illness, an emotional disturbance, a personality disorder, a communication disorder, a mental handicap, a social communication disorder, a developmental disability and more recently, an information processing problem, a movement disorder, or a sensory or perceptual condition and professionals of different sorts evolved from these camps.
>
> (p. 7)

To add to the complexities above, there is also the problem of how autism is understood in the public sphere – especially the media. It is almost impossible to pick up a newspaper and not be confronted with a news headline announcing the latest theory of autism. Many of these reports are pure sensationalism. The theories they publicise generally come and go quickly and are never heard of again. This is either because the research they are based upon is never replicated and confirmed and is therefore quickly forgotten – like the idea that autism is caused by too much television (Waldman et al. 2006), or because further analysis shows the research to be insubstantial, misleading or ill conceived in some way – like the idea that autism is caused by the MMR vaccination (Wakefield et al. 1998). A problem for the public is how to distinguish speculative claims from more authoritative research. Unfortunately, exposure in any of the media ensures that a variety of misunderstandings and misinformation about autism can be readily promulgated, largely without challenge. Many of these misunderstandings become lodged in the public imagination (Murray 2008). Practitioners, of course, are as vulnerable to these misunderstandings

as the next person, and may consciously or unconsciously draw upon them in their practice. Imagine the implications of this for the individuals they are supporting...

One of the most widespread and enduring myths of our times is that autism is characterised by severe and complex needs and exceptional skills. This myth probably has its origins in the 1980s blockbuster film *Rain Man*, which was one of the very first to take autism as its central theme. It was based upon the life of autistic savant, Kim Peake, who has classic Kanner autism and an exceptional mathematical ability. The presentation of autism in this film took a firm hold on the popular psyche and has been reinforced, subsequently, by a number of other films, books, documentaries and plays catering to a public utterly intrigued by the mystery of individuals with severe learning difficulties who can somehow draw, calculate or create with astonishing mastery. In fact, though the numbers continue to be contested (see Howlin et al. 2009), there is a wide consensus that these skills occur in less than 10% of the population with autism, so could not be said to be wholly representative of the condition. Yet, the association of autism with savant skills, and the more severe and complex form of the condition, remains highly resilient.

This can have deeply troubling consequences. For example, it may mean that some practitioners do not appreciate that there are individuals with autism who have a far more subtle, less visible form of the condition, known as High Functioning Autism (HFA) or Asperger's Syndrome (AS). Since autism is 'hidden' in these individuals, some practitioners simply dismiss their difficulties entirely or find alternative explanations for them that have nothing to do with autism. For instance, they might claim that an individual with HFA or AS is just being lazy or difficult, or has social, emotional and/ or behavioural difficulties. Such beliefs and responses severely disadvantage this group, making them especially vulnerable. We will return to this theme later on in the chapter.

The discussion above therefore sets the context. It tells us that, before we start to make sense of autism, we must be aware of what we may have already absorbed about the condition, possibly without even realising it. We may be harbouring myths and misunderstandings, or clinging to outdated 'truths'. We may also be influenced by research presented as 'fact' that might be better framed as hypothesis. We must therefore be cautious about *what we think we know*.

It is in this spirit that we proceed to the next section. Here we will continue to explore what autism is via a critical review of the key characteristics of the condition and the main theories that currently purport to explain it. What is presented here is, of necessity, a summary and a selection, since it is not within the limits of this chapter to provide a comprehensive overview. The main aim is to briefly clarify what autism is whilst problematising current theory and pinpointing the key controversies and ambiguities that practitioners face. We will see that understanding autism is not always easy.

The characteristics of autism: a triad of impairments?

From the moment Kanner and Asperger first applied the term 'autism', the race was on to identify the nuclear features of the condition that would enable the research community to identify its prevalence, determine its causes and develop medical, therapeutic and educational interventions to address it. Yet, despite a great deal of research from the early 1940s right through to the late 1970s, there was little agreement as to the core characteristics of the condition.

However, a major breakthrough came in 1979 when Lorna Wing and Judith Gould developed their triadic model of autism on the basis of the findings of their 'Camberwell Study' – a large-scale epidemiological study of 35,000 children with special needs under the age of 15 living in the Camberwell district in London (Wing & Gould 1979). Wing and Gould identified a group of children within this wider cohort who seemed to present with three distinct impairments corresponding very closely to the range of difficulties first identified by Kanner. They categorised these three features as:

- impairments of social communication
- impairments of social understanding
- impairments of imagination

Wing and Gould referred to these three features as the 'Triad of Impairments' – arguably the first succinct identification of the core characteristics of autism. It should be noted that the third area of the triad is now more commonly referred to as impairments of flexibility of thought and behaviour. This is a result of our growing understanding that people with autism do not necessarily lack imagination, but display a tendency towards narrow, repetitive and restrictive thinking, both imaginative and in general, which is linked to inflexible behaviour.

Wing and Gould made several further important observations during their study. They noted, for example, that there were three 'sub-types' within the group that interested them:

- one group of children showed the three core impairments accompanied by language difficulties and learning disability
- a second, larger group showed the three core impairments but had *no* language difficulties or learning disabilities
- and a third group showed one or two, but not all three, of the core impairments

These sub-types were subsequently identified as children with Autistic Disorder (AD), children with Asperger's Syndrome (AS) or High Functioning Autism (HFA), and children with Pervasive Developmental Disorder – Not Otherwise Specified (PDD-NOS) respectively. Whilst these sub-groups were distinguishable, Wing and Gould emphasised that the severity of the three core impairments seemed to vary from child to child across and within the sub-types. Thus, a highly able child with AS with no early language delay might nonetheless present with moderate difficulties with communication, social interaction and flexibility of thought, whilst another might have fewer communication and social interaction difficulties but complex problems with flexibility. The combinations vary from person to person. Wing and Gould also noted that a percentage of the children had co-morbid medical conditions such as epilepsy and Downs Syndrome. Other features, such as repetitive movements or 'stereotypies', exaggerated fears and anxieties, unusual gait and poor sensory integration, were also common across the sub-types.

Wing and Gould therefore highlighted the highly complex, variable and multidimensional nature of the condition. The variable features associated with autism are listed in box 1.2. Importantly, key strengths are also highlighted.

Box 1.2: The variable features of autism

Social communication

- No speech or restricted speech with much echolalia (echoing what is heard)
- Fluent speech but narrow and obsessive range of interests, topics of conversation plus idiosyncratic often dogmatic style (e.g. speaks *at* you)
- Problems with receptive communication, especially long instructions
- Problems interpreting facial expression and non-verbal communication
- Problems expressing feelings, personal information and choices
- Difficulties modulating and controlling pitch, rhythm and intonation of voice

Social interaction

- Difficulties understanding social rules and conventions
- Little interest in others as people, in the feelings of others or their point of view
- Problems with relationship formation
- Problems with social skills, e.g. working in a group, turn taking, listening to others, etc.
- Frequent failure to use social greetings
- Problems with imaginative play
- Difficulties with imitation and learning through observation

Flexibility of thought and behaviour

- Tendency to focus on details rather than wholes
- Strong preference for sameness and dislike of change
- May engage in repetitive self-stimulating behaviour, e.g. hand-flapping, staring at spinning objects
- May show restricted repetitive thinking, ritualistic behaviour and narrow range of interests
- Difficulties generalising and transferring knowledge and skills
- Problems with abstract concepts, e.g. time
- Failure to make links and see connections
- Difficulties stopping and starting and with transitions in general
- Tendency to be literal and 'black and white' in their thinking

Sensory processing

- May be hyper- (over) or hypo- (under) sensitive to smell, taste, touch, sound and visual stimuli
- There may be heightened or reduced sensitivity within the vestibular system (relating to bodily movement and position of the head), the proprioceptive system (relating to position in space) and to temperature and pain. May show associated motor disturbance, e.g. problems with fine motor skills such as writing, playing instruments, and gross motor skills such as sitting, running and skipping

Other issues

- Heightened fears and anxieties, e.g. fear of dogs, stairs, colours
- Lack of fear/dangerous behaviour
- Sleep disturbance
- Hyperactivity
- Eating problems
- Aggression and temper tantrums
- Self-injurious behaviour, e.g. head-banging

Strengths

- Logical thinkers (often good at puzzles)
- Scientific objectivity
- Good at categorising/organising information
- Strong focus (especially in areas of interest)
- Persistence
- Creative thinkers
- Visual acuity – eye for detail
- Good memory for facts

> • Can be highly gifted/talented (e.g. at performing calculations, drawing from memory)
> • Can show exceptional ability in areas of special interest
> (Based on Wing 1996, Dunlop et al. 2009)

Wing later proposed that autism should be conceptualised as a 'spectrum' of disorders (Wing 1996) that embraces this wide variety of manifestations, with severe Kanner autism at one end of the spectrum, and Asperger's Syndrome (AS) and High Functioning Autism (HFA) at the other.

Over subsequent years, Wing and Gould's triadic model of autism secured a broad consensus of support across the research community. It was also warmly welcomed by individuals with autism and their families, who found the notion of an autism spectrum accessible and meaningful (Wing 1996). Indeed, for the past 30 years, the idea of the triad of impairments has been the central, unifying principle that has underpinned our understanding of the behavioural manifestations of the condition and informed international diagnostic criteria.

However, this triadic model has been strongly challenged in recent years. Consider the following:

1   Boucher (2009) proposed that the triad of impairments should really be a dyad of impairments since, arguably, difficulties associated with social communication and social interaction are inextricably related to each other, i.e. they are 'not dissociable' (p. 89). They therefore belong in the same category. Thus, Boucher proposed a 'dyadic' model comprising a single category labelled 'social-interaction-communication impairments' coupled with 'impairments of behavioural flexibility' (ibid. p. 90).

2   Happe, Ronald and Plomin (2006) hypothesise that the three areas of the triad may not be linked or strongly correlated at all, but may have independent causes and separate developmental trajectories, i.e. they are 'fractionated'. Happe et al. therefore contest the fundamental principle of a triadic model and the assumed connections within it.

3   Several researchers, from Rimland (1964) to Bogdashina (2003), have proposed that sensory perception dysfunction is a core characteristic of autism, not merely an associated difficulty. They have therefore proposed that sensory perception dysfunction should be embedded into the triadic model, or placed in a fourth category, resulting in a quadratic model.

To date, the first and third of these proposals have gathered most support and have exerted a significant influence upon the literature and research.

In fact, they are now incorporated into the fifth revised set of international diagnostic criteria for autism, known as the *Diagnostic and Statistical Manual of Mental Disorders (DSM-5)*, mainly used in America. The previous version of this diagnostic, known as *DSM-IV*, was based squarely upon the Triad of Impairments. Sensory issues have never been listed as core diagnostic features of autism within this version, and the sub-types, like Asperger's Syndrome and PDD-NOS, have always been categorised separately.

The revised version, *DSM-5* has now been updated on the basis of the latest research. In the revised version, the three domains of the triadic model have been reduced to two domains, referred to as 'social/ communication deficits' and 'fixed interests and repetitive behaviours'. Arguments for a dyadic model have therefore proved persuasive. Sensory perceptual issues have been incorporated into the latter category and have therefore become central, rather than peripheral, to a diagnosis of autism – within this framework at least. Controversially, there are no longer separate diagnostic criteria for Asperger's Syndrome or PDD-NOS within the new framework, which effectively eliminates them as diagnostic categories. Thus, all sub-types are now viewed as 'variants of the same condition' and are subsumed under the broader umbrella of 'autism spectrum disorder'. Here we have an excellent illustration of the way that autism as a concept is constantly evolving.

Yet, confusingly, there is another set of diagnostic criteria, called the International Classification of Diseases (ICD), which is published by the World Health Organisation and used mainly in Britain. This classification system is still based upon the traditional triadic model of autism but is also due to be updated. It is not clear yet whether it will adopt the dyadic model and seek to harmonise with *DSM-5*. If not, it is possible that two different models will shortly be available simultaneously. Clearly, this could be confusing for practitioners – especially those involved in assessment and diagnosis. However, it should be noted that whether one uses the triadic or dyadic model, the key features of the condition remain the same, though with the latter there is greater emphasis on sensory issues.

For the purposes of this book, and in order to avoid confusion, autism will be defined as a complex neurodevelopmental condition, present from birth, and associated with mild, moderate or profound difficulties with communication, social interaction, flexibility of thought and behaviour and sensory integration. This definition reflects the broad consensus emerging within the current literature. However, by now we should be aware that autism is an 'evolving concept' (Roth 2010). Thus, it should not surprise us if future researchers contest and revise this definition.

Cognitive and affective theories of autism

Though Wing and Gould's triadic model of autism tells us what behaviours we might expect when interacting with an individual with autism, it does not *explain* the behaviours so that we can understand why they occur. Researchers have been keen to address this issue. The result is an ever-expanding variety of theories that attempt to provide a single, overarching explanation for the key features of autism. The main cognitive and affective theories, and their implications for everyday living, are summarised in box 1.3.

Box 1.3: The main theories of autism and their implications for everyday living

Theory of Mind Deficit (TOM) –
Baron-Cohen et al. (1985)

This theory suggests that people with autism may lack, or have weak 'Theory of Mind', i.e. the understanding that everyone has different thoughts, feelings, intentions and beliefs. This results in difficulties taking the perspective of another person.

Implications for everyday living

- Difficulty in predicting others' behaviour – fear and avoidance of others
- Difficulty reading the intentions and motives of others and understanding the motives behind their behaviour
- Difficulty in explaining own behaviour
- Difficulty in understanding emotions, their own and others', leading to a lack of empathy
- Difficulty understanding that behaviour affects how others think or feel – lack of conscience or motivation to please
- Difficulty taking into account what others know, or can be expected to know – pedantic or incomprehensible language
- Inability to read or react to listener's level of interest in what is being said
- Inability to anticipate what others might think of one's actions
- Inability to deceive or understand deception
- No shared attention, leading to idiosyncratic reference
- Lack of understanding of social interaction – turn taking, topic maintenance, inappropriate eye contact
- Difficulty in understanding 'pretend', or differentiating fact from fiction

Weak Central Coherence Theory – Frith (1989)

Frith explains the tendency of individuals with autism to focus on details rather than on the overall picture, and the related failure to draw information

---

together to construct high-level contextual meaning. This is linked to weak central coherence.

Implications for everyday living

- Idiosyncratic focus of attention
- Imposition of own perspective
- Preference for the known
- Inattentiveness to new tasks
- Difficulty in choosing and prioritising
- Difficulty in seeing connections and generalising skills and knowledge
- Lack of compliance

Executive Functioning Deficit – Ozonoff (1997)

Ozonoff suggests that individuals with autism have difficulties with executive skills such as planning and organising, behavioural flexibility, inhibiting inappropriate responses and generating new ideas. This is explained in relation to atypical executive functioning.

Implications for everyday living

- Behaviour is often rigid, inflexible and persevering
- Impulsive, having difficulty in holding back a response
- Often have a large store of knowledge but have difficulty applying it meaningfully
- Focus on detail and do not see the 'whole picture'
- Difficulties in perceiving emotion
- Difficulties in imitation
- Difficulties in pretend play
- Difficulty in planning
- Difficulty in starting and stopping

Theories of Affective Deficit – Hobson (1993)

Hobson proposes that people with autism have an innate inability to form emotional relationships with their primary care-giver and others from the moment of birth. This explains their lack of empathy and social development.

Implications for everyday living

- Lack of attachment
- Restricted eye contact
- Lack of interest in others
- Lack of empathy for the feelings of others
- Respond to people as objects
- Difficulty 'reading' facial expression and body language

- Tendency to believe that others have a similar mind and know what they think, feel, need, etc.
- Poor sense of 'self' as a separate identity, therefore poor personal memory
- Difficulty constructing personal 'meaning' in relation to experiences and events

Theories of Attention and Arousal Deficit – Murray et al. (2005)

This theory deals with the idea that individuals with autism have monotropic (single focus) rather than polytropic (multiple focus) attention. Some researchers argue that atypical attention may be linked to faulty arousal (under/over-arousal) and difficulty modulating arousal.

Implications for everyday living

- Idiosyncratic focus on, and response to, people, things and environments
- Difficulty learning new tasks
- Preference for sameness
- Lack of social responsiveness
- Lack of understanding of social contexts, self, others
- Problems with recognition
- Problems with joint attention
- Tendency to withdraw from arousing, complex environments
- Self-stimulatory behaviour (to block incoming stimuli)

Theories of Imitation – Williams et al. (2001)

Williams et al. argue that since imitation plays a vital role in typical child development and is also essential to children's play, a lack of imitation, or impaired imitation (as in echolalia), is likely to seriously undermine social development and learning in general. They link imitation problems to disturbances of the mirror neuron system.

Implications for everyday living

- Poor social communication and social understanding
- Lack of TOM
- Learning difficulties
- Impact on pretend and functional play
- Poor development of affective expression

A number of points can be made about these theories:

1   Firstly, it is important to note that, to date, no single theory has explained the entire range of behaviours associated with autism. Indeed, Schreibman (2005) points out that none of them currently meets the four criteria necessary and sufficient for a 'core' theory of autism:
    ○   universality – it applies in every case
    ○   specificity – it is distinct to autism and not to any other condition
    ○   precedence – it begins at birth
    ○   persistence – it is present across the lifespan
    Rather, each theory explains some aspects of behaviour, often with a degree of overlap with other theories. Indeed, it is only in conjunction with each other that a comprehensive explanation can be achieved. So, for example, whilst lack of Theory of Mind (TOM) might explain why individuals with autism find it difficult to take the perspective of another person, this does not explain other autistic traits like insistence on routine and 'sameness', narrow focus and literal interpretation. It is necessary to turn to other theories to address this gap. Thus, each of these theories has limited scope.
2   It ought to be emphasised that not all aspects of these theories are directly testable (as yet), i.e. they are working hypotheses. For example, Executive Functioning Deficit theory claims to explain repetitive behaviours like hand-flapping. However, as Roth (2010) points out, no test has been developed to directly evidence this link.
3   The overlap between different theories can create difficulties. How are service practitioners to know, for example, whether TOM is a better explanation for poor perspective taking than Hobson's affective theory? Similarly, is attention deficit theory a more accurate explanation of monotropism than central coherence deficit theory? How do we know? A key problem for practitioners is therefore navigating this wide range of theory and being able to apply it.

There is a great deal of ongoing research into theories of autism and there is clearly much scope for the improvement and refinement of existing theories. Nonetheless, their current value, when taken together, lies in their explanatory power. Arguably, they have enabled us to gain significant insights into the workings of the autistic mind by casting light on how and why individuals with autism have such a very different way of framing the world – one that lies outside common experience. Indeed, it is precisely because it lies outside common experience that 'neurotypical' individuals (i.e. those who do *not* have autism) can find it so difficult to grasp this unique perceptual style. The fact that autism, at the more subtle end of the spectrum, is a 'hidden' difference not immediately obvious to the observer, only serves to exacerbate this problem. Indeed, some researchers therefore argue that whilst individuals with autism lack theory of *neurotypical* mind, equally, neurotypical individuals lack theory of *autistic* mind (Bogdashina 2010). In other words the difficulty is mutual; we are equally alien to each other.

This perception gap between the neurotypical mind and the autistic mind has profound implications. It means that practitioners must take an intuitive leap if they are to understand autism, and an imaginative leap if they are to enter the autistic world. Yet it is only by doing so that practitioners can identify individual needs and provide the individualised support and interventions that clients require. Some practitioners find this extremely stressful and challenging, yet others find it highly stimulating and rewarding. Indeed, research indicates that practitioners who are highly effective in their work with clients with autism tend to possess a range of common attributes that are, in many respects, the opposite of autistic features. Successful practitioners are usually 'mental adventurers – attracted to the unknown' (Smith 2011, p. 44) and are highly adaptable, flexible, enquiring, empathetic, determined and, often, rather unorthodox people (ibid.). It is not clear whether these are innate personality traits or attributes that develop and grow through the experience of working with individuals with autism – perhaps it is a mixture of both. Nonetheless, this research seems to be telling us that understanding autism is easier for some than others. This clearly has implications for workplace recruitment.

Summary

The discussion above has explored what autism is and has clarified the characteristics of the condition and how these might be explained. In doing so, it has highlighted the complexity arising from the diverse cultural influences that shape our understanding of autism, and the ambiguities that arise from competing models and theories. It has also highlighted the challenge of autism to our taken-for-granted beliefs and assumptions about what is 'normal', and to our capacity to conceive of different ways of thinking, learning and being in the world. It is therefore with good reason that autism is often referred to as a 'puzzle' in the literature. However, it is a puzzle from which we can learn as much about ourselves as human beings as we can about autism. The puzzle of autism is therefore the puzzle of what it means to be human in all its richness (McGuire & Michalko 2011).

The ambiguity and complexity associated with autism, and the difficulty, for practitioners, of grasping its meaning accounts, in part, for the very slow evolution of suitably adapted service provision. Unfortunately, when we consider autism in an inclusive context, this complexity is compounded. In the next section we will explore why.

Note

1   The word 'autism' is used generically to refer to Kanner Autism, Asperger's Syndrome and High Functioning Autism.

References

Allely, C.S., Gillberg, C. & Wilson, P. (2013) Neurobiological abnormalities in the first few years of life in individuals later diagnosed with Autism Spectrum Disorder: a review of recent data, *Behavioural Neurology*, 2014, 141–160.

Asperger, H. (1944) Die 'aunstisehen Psychopathen' im Kindesalter, *Archiv fur psychiatrie und* Nervenkrankheiten, 117, 76–136.

Baron-Cohen, S. (2000) Is Asperger syndrome/high functioning autism necessarily a disability? *Development & Psychopathology*, 12, 489–500.

Baron-Cohen, S., Leslie, A.M. & Frith, U. (1985) Does the autistic child have a 'Theory of Mind'?, *Cognition*, 21/1, 37–46.

Baron-Cohen, S., Scott, F.J., Allison, C., Williams, J., Bolton, P., Mathews, F.E. & Brayne, C. (2009) Prevalence of Autism Spectrum Conditions: UK school-based population study, *British Journal of Psychiatry*, 194, 500–519.

Bettleheim, B. (1967) *The Empty Fortress: Infantile Autism and the Birth of the Self*, New York: The Free Press.

Bogdashina, O. (2003) *Sensory Perceptual Issues in Autism and Asperger Syndrome*, London: Jessica Kingsley.

Bogdashina, O. (2010) *Autism and the Edges of the Known World: Sensitivities, Language and Constructed Reality*, London: Jessica Kingsley.

Boucher, J. (2009) *The Autistic Spectrum: Characteristics, Causes and Practical Issues*, London: Sage.

Broek, J.A.C., Guest, P.C., Rahmoune, H. & Bahn, S. (2014) Proteomic analysis of *post mortem* brain tissue from autism patients: evidence for opposite changes in prefrontal cortex and cerebellum in synaptic connectivity-related proteins, *Molecular Autism*, 5/41, 1–8.

Courchesne, E. (2004) Brain development in autism: early overgrowth followed by premature arrest of growth, *Mental Retardation and Developmental Disabilities Research Review*, 10, 106–111.

Courchesne, E. & Pierce, K. (2005) Why the frontal cortex in autism might be talking only to itself: Local over-connectivity but long distance disconnection, *Current Opinion in Neurobiology*, 15, 225–230.

Courchesne, E., Campbell, K. & Solso, S. (2011) Brain growth across the life span in autism: Age-specific changes in anatomical pathology, *Brain Research*, 1380, 138–145.

Dunlop, A.-W., Tait, C., Leask, A., Glashan, L., Robinson, A. & Marwick, H. (2009) *The Autism Toolbox: An autism resource for Scottish Schools*, Edinburgh: Scottish Government.

Edmonson, C., Ziats, M.N. & Rennert, O.M. (2014) Altered glial marker expression in autistic post-mortem prefrontal cortex and cerebellum, *Molecular Autism*, 5/3, 1–9.

Frith, U. (1989) *Autism: Explaining the Enigma*, Oxford: Blackwell.

Gerber, J.S. & Offit, P.A. (2009) Vaccines & autism: a tale of shifting hypotheses, *Clinical Infectious Diseases*, 48/4, 456–461.

Gillberg, C. & Gillberg, C. (1989) Asperger Syndrome – some epidemiological considerations: a research note, *Journal of Child Psychology and Psychiatry*, 30/4, 631–638.

Happe, F., Ronald, A. & Plomin R. (2006) Time to give up on a single explanation for autism, *Nature Neuroscience*, 9, 1218–1220.

Hilton, S., Hunt, K. & Petticrew, M. (2007) MMR: Marginalised, misrepresented and rejected? Autism: a focus group study, *Archives of Disease in Childhood*, 92/4, 322–327.

Hobson, P.R. (1993) *Autism and the Development of Mind*, London: Taylor & Francis.

Howlin, P., Goode, S., Hutton, J. & Rutter, M. (2009) Savant skills in autism: psychometric approaches and parental reports, *Philosophical Transactions of the Royal Society B*, 364, 1359–1367.

Just, M.A., Cherkassky, V.L., Keller, T.A., Kana, K.K. & Minshew, N.J. (2007) Functional and anatomical cortical underconnectivity in autism: evidence from an fMRI study of an executive function task and corpus callosum morphometry, *Cerebral Cortex*, 17/4, 951–961.

Kanner, L. (1943). Autistic disturbances of affective contact, *Nervous Child*, 2, 217–250.

Lathe, R. (2006) *Autism, Brain and Environment*, London: Jessica Kingsley.

McGuire, A.E. & Michalko, R. (2011) Minds between us: autism, mindblindness and the uncertainty of communication, *Educational Philosophy and Theory*, 43/2, 162–177.

Mockett, M., Hackett, L., Theodosiou, L., Hackett, R. & Mockett, A. (2009) A study into the beliefs relating to causation and the autism spectrum within Asian and White British families living in Manchester, *Good Autism Practice*, 10/2, 64–75.

Muller, R.-A., (2007) The study of autism as a distributed disorder, *Mental Retardation and Developmental Disabilities Research Reviews*, 13, 85–95.

Murray, D., Lesser, M. & Lawson, W. (2005) Attention, monotropism and the diagnostic criteria for autism, *Autism*, 9/2, 139–156.

Murray, S. (2008) *Representing Autism: Culture, Narrative, Fascination*, Liverpool: Liverpool University Press.

Ozonoff, S. (1997). Components of executive function in autism and other disorders, in J. Russell (ed.), *Autism as an Executive Disorder* (pp. 179–211). Oxford: Oxford University Press.

Rimland, B. (1964) *Infantile Autism: The Syndrome and its Implications for a Neural Theory of Behaviour*, East Norwalk, CT: Appleton-Century-Crofts.

Roth, I. (2010) *The Autism Spectrum in the 21st Century*, London: Jessica Kingsley.

Rutter, M., Bartak, L. & Newman, S. (1971) Autism – a central disorder of cognition and language? In M. Rutter (ed.), *Infantile Autism: Concepts, Characteristics and Treatment* (pp. 148–171). London: Churchill Livingstone.

Schreibman L. (2005) *The Science and Fiction of Autism*, London: Harvard University Press.

Smith, J.A. (2011) Mutual Attraction? How do we identify and attract the right people to work in the field of autism? *Good Autism Practice*, 12/2, 43–50.

Soklowski, K. & Corbin, J.G. (2012) Wired for behaviours: from development to function of innate limbic system circuitry, *Frontiers in Molecular Neuroscience*, 5/55, 1–15.

Taylor Dyches, T., Wilder, L.K., Sudweeks, R.R., Obiakor, F.E. & Algozzine, B. (2004) Multicultural issues in autism, *Journal of Autism & Developmental Disorders*, 34/2, 211–222.

Wakefield, A., Murch, S., Anthony, A. et al. (1998) Ileal-lymphoid-nodular hyperplasia, non-specific colitis, and pervasive developmental disorder in children, *Lancet*, 351/9103, 637–641.

Waldman, M., Nicholson, S. & Adilov, N. (2006). Does television cause autism? *NBER Working Paper No. 12632*. Accessible: http://www.nber.org/papers/w12632 (accessed July 2014).

Williams, D. (1997) *Autism: An Inside-Out Approach*, London: Jessica Kingsley.

Williams, J.H.G., Whitten, A., Suddendorf, T. & Perrett, D.I. (2001) Imitation, motor neurons and autism, *Neuroscience and Behavioural Review*, 25, 287–295.

Wing, L. (1981) Asperger's Syndrome: a clinical account, *Psychological Medicine*, 11/1, 115–129.

Wing, L. (1996) *The Autistic Spectrum: A Guide for Parents and Professionals*, London: Constable.

Wing, L. & Gould, J. (1979) Severe impairments of social interaction and associated abnormalities in children: Epidemiology and classification, *Journal of Autism and Childhood Schizophrenia*, 9, 11–29.

Chapter 2

Understanding autism in an inclusive context

The concept of inclusion lies at the heart of UK social and educational policy and has done so for well over a decade. It is a concept that is notoriously difficult to define since, like our concept of autism, it means different things to different people in different contexts and is also constantly evolving over time (Parry et al. 2010). However, for the purposes of this book, inclusion is taken to mean increasing access and participation for all by bringing an end to the various forms of segregation and exclusion that for many years have marginalised large sections of the population on the basis of race, gender, sexual orientation, ethnicity, religion and/or disability. Such a transformation implies structural and attitudinal, as well as practice changes within the workplace. These changes rely, in turn, on wider socio-political and cultural transformations based on the ideals of social justice, social equality and democratic participation (Griffiths 2003).

Over the years, a raft of policy and guidance documents have been published to advance the notion of inclusion and to embed autism and inclusive practice across service settings. Some have been autism specific (e.g. PHIS 2001, DoH 2006, HMIE 2006, NAS 2007, Scottish Government 2008, DCSF 2009) and have had the singular aim of enhancing inclusion for the estimated 700,000 individuals with autism in the UK (NAS 2014). On the face of it, people with autism and their families should, by now, be starting to enjoy the benefits of the sustained political drive towards a fairer and more inclusive society for all. Yet, there is clear and unequivocal evidence, highlighted in the introduction to this book, that significant numbers of children, young people and adults with autism continue to experience exclusion and marginalisation across UK services.

Why?

In seeking to answer this question, we will start by considering more deeply the meaning of inclusion by exploring two contrasting discourses on the subject. Throughout this discussion we will examine how competing and contradictory interpretations of inclusion create dilemmas for practitioners that can undermine autism practice and provision. When these are added to the many controversies and ambiguities already discussed in chapter 1, we begin to understand the complexities that confront practitioners in the workplace before they even begin the practical task of transforming theory into practice.

Inclusion and autism

Inclusion, like autism, is a highly contested concept. Though the principle itself is rarely disputed (few would argue against the desirability of an equal, just and democratic society for all), the way that the concept is interpreted, and then enacted, varies widely across service contexts, within individual workplaces and at the level of individual professional practice. This variation depends, of course, on a complex range of individual, environmental and socio-cultural factors that it is not within the limits of this chapter to explore. However, arguably, the various ways that inclusion is discussed in the workplace and written about in the literature are likely to exert a highly potent influence. It is to these 'cultural discourses' on inclusion that we now turn.

Inclusion discourses are ubiquitous, though we may not be fully aware of them. They have the power to shape perceptions, attitudes and professional practice (Allan 2008). Allan points out that there are a number of different and, often, competing discourses on inclusion in educational contexts and she argues that this accounts for the incoherence and inconsistency that characterises much inclusive practice in schools (ibid.). Arguably, this is also true of inclusion within the health and social care sectors.

In order to make better sense of this problem as it applies to individuals with autism, I will discuss two contrasting discourses within the current inclusion debate. The first will be referred to as the 'rights-based discourse'; the second will be referred to as the 'needs-based discourse'. The aim of this section is to pinpoint the key features of these competing discourses, and to explore why they cause confusion for practitioners and undermine service provision.

Inclusion discourses: rights versus needs

Simply put, the rights-based inclusion discourse is based on the premise that all individuals have a basic human right to full participation in all aspects of mainstream culture and society alongside peers, and that diversity, in its multitude of forms, should be welcomed, celebrated and explicitly catered for. Thus, a 'presumption of mainstreaming' and the transformation of mainstream institutional structures and processes to accommodate full inclusion are foregrounded within this perspective. Medical labelling and segregated specialist provision are considered discriminatory and exclusionist.

By contrast, the needs-based inclusion discourse is based on the premise that all individuals should have their needs identified and met in a context that is fully accessible, fully adapted and, where necessary, specialised. Thus access to a medical diagnosis and specialist provision are foregrounded within this perspective and the emphasis on the overriding importance of mainstreaming is questioned. Indeed, mainstreaming is associated with a 'one size fits all' approach that overlooks individual needs and leads to marginalisation and exclusion.

It is not difficult to see that, on the surface at least, these two discourses are diametrically opposed. Indeed, bipolar thinking and strong moral posturing are characteristic of the two discourses (Allan 2008). Unfortunately, this is deeply confusing for practitioners supporting individuals with autism, for it inevitably results in an uncomfortable professional dilemma: 'Do I to treat everyone the same or do I respond to difference?' Both horns of the dilemma are inclusionary or exclusionary, depending on which discourse one subscribes to. This creates a fundamental practice dichotomy that is widely recognised within the inclusion literature (Dyson 2005, Norwich 2007).

Let us, therefore, examine this dilemma more closely. To illustrate it, we will discuss the issues that arise when the rights-based and needs-based perspectives on inclusion are applied to medical labelling and specialist approaches as they relate to autism. Both of these practices are considered exclusionary under the rights-based approach, but inclusionary under the needs-based approach, and can therefore trap practitioners in uncertainty and paralysis. We will begin by identifying the key arguments that underpin the two positions and that tend to reinforce bipolar thinking. We will then consider whether there is any middle ground that the two positions could be said to share. In doing so, we will begin to see how inclusion dilemmas may have some possibility of resolution. Indeed, I propose a 'third way' which I refer to as an 'integrative position'.

Dilemmas linked to medical labelling

Rights-based inclusionists argue that medical categories, like autism, cannot simply be accepted as objective, universal 'truths', but might be more accurately described as 'constructions' that arise in particular socio-cultural contexts, at particular historical moments, based on the underlying assumptions and beliefs of the times (Graham 2006). These constructions then become 'reified' or treated like 'facts', and are solidified further as they are linked to specific identities (ibid.). In the case of autism, these identities are pathologised, associated with 'impairment' and disorder', and become leaden with negative beliefs about restricted abilities and limited potential (Gillman et al. 2000). A deficit model of the individual then ensues (Thomas & Loxley 2007) that locates the 'problem of autism' within the individual rather than in the wider environment around them, leading to blame, low expectations, social and academic exclusion and the use of 'normalising' interventions to 'correct' disability. A 'personal tragedy' perspective can be superimposed on to the autism identity, which may negatively influence outcomes and compound marginalisation and exclusion (Ho 2004).

For rights-based inclusionists, the solution to this catalogue of negativity is the rejection of the medical model of disability – especially notions of 'impairment'. A social model of disability is proposed instead that shifts our gaze away from individuals with autism as pathologised and excluded 'bodies', and focuses instead upon the problem of pathologising and exclusionary 'environments' and institutions (Goodley & Runswick-Cole 2011). In other words, the deficit is located in the context, not in the individual with autism. Though it is acknowledged that a diagnosis may be necessary, the value of medical labels beyond medical contexts is questioned. Thus, the use of words like 'autistic' to describe individuals on the spectrum is avoided wherever possible. Where necessary, they are replaced with more careful and respectful phrases like 'person with autism', that disassociate the condition from personal identity (Ho 2004).

By contrast, needs-based inclusionists strongly defend the value of a medical diagnosis and label both within and beyond medical contexts for several reasons. Clearly, a diagnosis enables individuals with autism, their families and the professionals supporting them to make sense of the condition and understand its complex, and often subtle, manifestations. This is crucial, because autism can be puzzling, distressing and very difficult to cope with both for those with a diagnosis and those around them. However, a medical label alerts others in the community to this. A medical assessment also draws attention to individual strengths and talents so that these can be developed and capitalised upon. A medical label should therefore be associated with these strengths, as well as with the inevitable challenges, and should play a positive role in drawing attention to them. This enables those supporting individuals with autism to create packages of support to meet individual requirements that build on strengths in order to reduce the impact of the condition. Furthermore, a medical label brings legal and financial support that could not otherwise be accessed (Ho 2004). All this can only happen where 'difference is recognised' (Graham 2006).

Similarly, the idea that the word 'autistic' is somehow disrespectful is not always accepted by needs-based inclusionists. Indeed, it is argued that many individuals with autism are proud to be autistic and do not wish to be disassociated from their condition as if it is somehow 'shameful' (Cigman 2007, p. xxxvi):

> I am not a 'person with autism'. I am an autistic person… Saying 'person with autism' suggests that autism is something bad – so bad that it isn't even consistent with being a person.
>
> (Sinclair 1998 in Cigman 2007, p. xxvi)

Thus, paradoxically, medical labelling can be argued to be both exclusionary and inclusionary. On the one hand it is exclusionary because it draws attention to difference and invites negative beliefs which can result in marginalisation. On the other hand, it is inclusionary because it supports recognition and acceptance of difference and draws attention to individual strengths as well as needs, which can result in greater participation.

Looked at this way, the polarisation of the two positions is total. However, the problem with these two discourses is that they tend to over-simplify their underpinning values and beliefs, and over-state the differences that divide them. Things are not as black and white as they seem if commonalities are taken into consideration. The problem is that these commonalities are rarely discussed in the literature and are not widely recognised. This is singularly unhelpful and simply ensures that practice dilemmas are never resolved. We will therefore briefly consider where the two discourses converge.

Rights and needs: commonalities linked to medical labelling

1   Whilst needs-based inclusionists assert the importance of medical diagnoses and the utility of medical labelling, they agree with rights-based inclusionists that the medical model is problematic (Frith 1991, Molloy & Vasil 2004). For example, it would be difficult to deny that autism, as a medical category, is in constant flux and is highly contested. The notion of autism as a fixed, objective certainty (Gillman et al. 2000) has therefore come under scrutiny, whilst the notion of autism as a 'constructed' category is becoming much more widely accepted, as was discussed in some detail in chapter 1. It follows, therefore, that autism as a medical category might be more usefully regarded as a working hypothesis than a fixed entity. Even autism researchers within the medical sciences (Williams 2014) are moving beyond strict adherence to a medical model. Many of these researchers simply cannot assume the validity of the medical model, especially when working within a collaborative context where such assumptions are increasingly contested. Some convergence of the two perspectives is therefore beginning to develop.

2   Whilst needs-based inclusionists argue that medical labels are vital, there is nonetheless a growing determination to problematise their use, especially the practice of categorising autism as an 'impairment' or 'disorder' (Frith 1991). Indeed, it has been widely suggested over recent years that the full range of what are currently referred to as 'autism spectrum disorders' might be re-categorised as neurological *differences* associated with a unique profile of strengths as well as challenges (Baron-Cohen 2000). Jordan (2006) has proposed that the notion of autism spectrum disorder might be changed to 'autism spectrum condition' – the term used throughout this book. Lawson (2008) argues

that the notion of disability might be changed to 'diffability'. The power of language to shape thinking and behaviour is being addressed here, with the hope that these alternative labels might subvert negative and limited thinking about individuals with autism.

However, whilst the idea of autism as a neurological 'difference' might be viewed as a much more positive way of distinguishing the condition, the notion itself raises the question: 'Different to what?' and poses the associated problem of distinguishing 'different' from 'not different' and establishing the fine line between the two. After all, everyone, in a sense, is neurologically unique. Using the term 'difference' might therefore reduce the impact of negative labelling, but it does not fully resolve the problems that words create.

It might also be argued that the notion of autism as a 'difference' is inappropriate in cases where autism is accompanied by severe and complex difficulties, co-morbid conditions and/or physical and mental health problems. Boucher (2009) points out that the parents and carers of children and young people experiencing such multiple difficulties do not see their children as 'merely different' (p. 39). She makes the important point that we cannot value diversity by simply 'underplaying, essentially denying' (ibid.) the seriousness of the condition some individuals face. There is a fear that if we re-categorise autism as a 'difference', it might be taken less seriously and may be approached with less urgency and rigour.

Though a consensus has not yet emerged on these matters, the existence of the debate is highly significant and might be considered representative of the shift from an 'autism as disease' metaphor to an emerging 'autism as neurodiversity' metaphor that has gathered wide support over recent years (Broderick & Ne'eman 2008). This counter-narrative signals a determination to shift perceptions and attitudes away from a medical, deficit model towards greater respect for, and acceptance of, those with autism (ibid.), and greater recognition of their strengths. The needs-based and rights-based perspectives have much in common within this debate and share the same motivation to reduce discriminatory attitudes towards autism and other disabilities.

The discussion above therefore clarifies the essential contradictions, as well as the key commonalities, which characterise the two perspectives on medical labelling. Unfortunately, these commonalities are rarely identified or explained in the literature and therefore remain invisible within the autism and inclusion debate, reinforcing the theoretical divide. By bringing them more squarely into view, an 'integrative' position begins to emerge that undermines the power of the binary and represents a significant step forward for the inclusion debate. Box 2.1(a) clarifies this by summarising the key features of the rights-based, needs-based and integrative perspectives on autism, inclusion and medical labelling.

Box 2.1: Summary of key features of contradictory perspectives highlighting binary oppositions and integrative perspective

	Rights-based perspective	Needs-based perspective	Integrative perspective
a) Medical labelling	Social model	Medical model/ Social Model	Social model (Medical *Hypothesis* model)
	Values right to be the same, avoids reifying difference	Values right to be different, avoids 'one size fits all'	Seeks balance of rights
	Labelling negative and exclusionary	Labelling confirming, useful and inclusionary	Seeks to minimise negative labelling and exclusion by rejecting 'autism as disease' metaphor
			Seeks to maximise inclusion by valuing neurodiversity
b) Special pedagogies	Exclusionary – reinforces difference, consolidates medical determinism	Inclusionary – clarifies difference, challenges neurotypical determinism	Seeks to minimise both medical and neurotypical determinism
	Autism pedagogies not 'special', 'different from' or 'additional to' but 'common to all' (unique differences position)	Autism pedagogies are 'special' (linked to specific group needs), 'different from' and 'additional to' (general differences position)	Autism pedagogies are distinct (cannot be 'intuited') but neither 'special' nor 'common to all'. Other children may benefit
	Advocates single 'inclusion' pedagogy for all learners. Highlights exclusionary potential of special pedagogies	Advocates 'special pedagogies' for learners with autism. Highlights exclusionary potential of 'one size fits all'	Advocates 'distinct' autism pedagogy to complement inclusion pedagogy, meet group needs and avoid risk of exclusion
	No need for autism training	Need specially trained autism teachers	Need whole-school autism awareness and autism training for *all* staff
	No need for segregated autism provision, all learners taught in mainstream classrooms	Need adapted, responsive segregated autism provision for some learners	All schools should be 'autism friendly' with range of provision to meet range of group needs

Dilemmas concerning specialist approaches

Specialist approaches are modes of instruction 'informed by needs that are specific or distinctive to a group that shares common characteristics' (Lewis & Norwich 2005, p. 3). The dilemma we are examining in this section is therefore about whether there are particular ways of supporting individuals with autism that are, in some way, distinct and reliant on specialist training, insight and know-how. If they are not distinct, then there would be little need for practitioners to have an awareness and understanding of autism or knowledge of specific forms of intervention. If they are distinct, then there is a case for specialist training. So this is a crucial debate for practitioners, service providers and individuals with autism.

As a result of the link to instruction in the definition above, much of the literature I will refer to in this section will come largely from educational research. However, this does not mean that it is only relevant to practitioners in an educational context, since we are concerned with instruction in its widest sense. Thus, this discussion will be pertinent to how occupational therapists support adults with autism to organise a trip to the cinema or handle money, or how parents support a child's dressing routine or a visit to the dentist. All of these scenarios are 'educational' in the sense that the practitioner/parent is involved in teaching the individual with autism something new. Rights-based and needs-based inclusionists have a very different understanding of the necessity of specialist approaches in these sorts of scenarios. We will consider the rights-based perspective first.

Simply put, rights-based inclusionists make two key arguments *against* the use of specialist approaches.

The 'anti-specialist' argument

Firstly, it is argued that specialist approaches, by their very nature, imply that general practitioners cannot teach this group without 'expertise' (Florian 2007), for they consolidate the notion that individuals with autism require 'specialist' practitioners in 'special' contexts (ibid.). This can have the unfortunate outcome of enabling untrained practitioners to absolve themselves of all responsibility for supporting individuals with autism, and clearly has the potential to reinforce exclusionary practices in any service context. Furthermore, a range of research suggests that what is 'special' about specialist approaches is not so much the content of the instruction (what you are teaching) or the technique (how you teach it) – which, it is argued, is the same for all learners – but the way it is delivered or applied to individual learners (Carlberg & Kavale 1980, Cook & Schirmer 2003, Davis & Florian 2004, Lewis & Norwich 2005, Florian 2007). If this is the case, then the approaches themselves are not specialist at all, and are no different to those generally and widely used with other learners, i.e. they

'...are relevant or effective for all...irrespective of social background, ethnicity, gender and disability' (Norwich & Lewis 2005, pp. 3–4). It therefore follows that any practitioner is quite capable of applying them.

The 'common to all' argument

Secondly, rights-based inclusionists argue that the needs associated with learners with autism are not unique but shared by many other learners who are not on the spectrum. These learners may not have medical conditions, but they nonetheless experience difficulties with certain aspects of communication, social interaction or flexibility of thought and imagination (Davis & Florian 2004). For example, many individuals have problems understanding turn-taking, social rules, relationship formation and flexibility at times of change or transition, just like individuals with autism. Inclusionists subscribing to this argument therefore reject the notion that there are distinct sub-groups of learners, and focus instead on what is 'common to all' (ibid.).

Applied to autism, the logic of the above argument leads to the conclusion that there is no case for recognising individuals with autism as a distinct group since they have things in common with all learners and also they do not require to be taught anything that is 'different from or additional to' any other group (Florian 2007 p. 15). Picking out individuals with autism for 'specialist' treatment is therefore viewed as discriminatory and is considered to create marginalisation and exclusion.

Needs-based inclusionists disagree with this argument. Their counter-argument might proceed as follows:

Response to the anti-specialist argument

Needs-based inclusionists fundamentally agree that *what* is taught, and the approaches and techniques used to teach it, will inevitably be common to all. However, they emphasise that it is *how* and *why* particular techniques are applied to individual learners with autism that is crucial and distinctive, for this relies on a level of understanding of the condition. Attaining this level of understanding, in turn, calls for a level of specialism. For example, they argue that practitioners must have specific training in autism in order to be able to make sense of learner behaviour and responses in the learning context and to identify and assess specific needs in the first place. Practitioners must then draw on their understanding of the condition to adapt the environment, approaches and interventions in order to meet those individual needs effectively (Jones et al. 2008). It does not matter that these approaches and techniques are also used with other service users who do not have autism; what matters is the way that instruction is filtered and transformed by drawing on a knowledge of autism – referred to as 'using the autism lens'. If a practitioner lacks this lens, they will not be able to support the learner with autism effectively. This argument is further developed in the section below.

Response to the 'common to all' argument

Jordan (2005) concedes that learners with autism have individual needs like many other learners and also needs in common with all learners. However, she argues that, additionally, they have a unique configuration of needs that combine, when experienced together at a particular level of severity, to significantly influence their general development and to satisfy a diagnosis of autism. This is obviously not true of learners who have mild characteristics of some features of the triad of impairments and no diagnosis of autism or any other condition.

For example, learners with English as a foreign language have problems understanding idioms. It is widely recognised that this is also a common problem for learners with autism. However, though these two groups have the same presenting problem, this does not mean that they have the same underlying difficulty – indeed, it would be highly misleading to assume so and would significantly subvert the teaching and learning process. The problem is that practitioners with no training in autism are likely to fall into this trap since the underlying difficulty is not something you can observe or 'intuit'. Indeed it is precisely the *appearance of commonality* that seduces many practitioners to treat everyone the same. Since this is important, let us explore this matter a little more deeply.

Clearly, English language learners do not grasp common idioms because of their very weak grasp of the structure and vocabulary of their second language. However, when they are taught this structure and vocabulary, and introduced to the concept of idioms, they can quickly recognise an idiom when they read it or hear it and then learn how to use it appropriately. This is not the case for learners with autism, including those with outstanding superficial language fluency. This group tend to have an atypical grasp of language and communication which is linked to an underlying difference in processing style (Baron-Cohen 2003). Simply put, they tend to interpret language literally (Schreibman 2005) and therefore read metaphorical language as if it can be taken at face value. Thus, if a learner on the spectrum is told to pull their socks up, this may be exactly what they do. Further, since they have a tendency towards monotropic attention (see chapter 1), they frequently fail to grasp the overall meaning of text and speech, and, consequently, do not notice that their literal interpretation makes little sense. Clearly, the underlying reason for the problem with idioms in each group is completely different. Any intervention that follows must be completely different too.

The practitioner with autism training would grasp these underlying differences immediately by using the 'autism lens', i.e. by filtering surface behaviours through a knowledge and understanding of autism. However, the untrained practitioner cannot perceive these underlying differences since they only have access to the 'neurotypical lens', i.e. their judgment is only informed by their understanding of typical development and common forms of learning. This results in a tendency to treat all learners the same. Such practitioners may never become aware of the many, often subtle, ways in which their practice may be directly limiting and undermining the learning and progress of clients with autism. Unfortunately, stress, marginalisation and exclusion are the likely outcomes for many of those clients.

This example helps to clarify why needs-based inclusionists insist on autism training for all service practitioners (McKay & Dunlop 2004). It also explains why it can be damaging to make a simplistic comparison between the needs of individuals with autism and the needs of individuals with what appear to be 'autism-like' difficulties. For this reason Jordan (2005) concludes that those with autism are a distinct group who need an 'individualised approach informed by understanding of ASDs' (p. 118).

Having said this, needs-based inclusionists acknowledge that this 'distinct group' position can create problems. They acknowledge, for example, that it may persuade some practitioners that they are not capable of supporting individuals with autism and reinforces a tendency to assume that a specialist context is necessary for this group (Jones et al. 2008). This is far from the case, since many individuals with autism can thrive in mainstream contexts providing they have sensitive and appropriate support (Humphrey & Lewis 2008). On the other hand, it can further entrench some practitioners in a 'one size fits all' position, and the attitude that it is clients with autism who must adapt and conform to the context, not practitioners. Research suggests that exclusion levels are high where this attitude prevails (ibid.). In the middle of these two positions are likely to be many practitioners who are simply confused and undecided.

One way around this polarised, black and white thinking is to propose that all practitioners, through professional training, should have a minimal awareness of autism spectrum condition (McKay & Dunlop 2004). Those working directly with individuals with autism should have higher levels of training in order to meet their responsibilities for inclusion (ibid.). This is an alternative and more 'integrative' position that seeks to ensure that all environments, approaches and interventions are suitably adapted to enable those with autism to participate and succeed in any context. The key features of this integrative position in relation to the rights-based and needs-based perspectives on special pedagogies are summarised in box 2.1(b).

The idea that practitioners across service contexts require training in autism has recently begun to receive much wider acknowledgement and greater acceptance on the basis of recent research (Batten & Daly 2006, Batten et al. 2006, Dunlop et al. 2009). It is notable that this demand is echoed in recent national autism initiatives (Autism Act 2009, Scottish

Government 2011) and is a recurring theme across national policy guidance (HMIE 2006, SIGN 2007).

Summary

This chapter set out to explain some of the underlying factors that explain the woefully slow progress in the development of effective, inclusive provision for individuals with autism. The focus has been on some of the complex theoretical issues – the controversies and dilemmas – that underpin this failure, linked to two key contradictory discourses on inclusion: the rights-based discourse and needs-based discourse. The profound shaping influence of these underpinning discourses, and their potential to skew and obscure professional practice, has been our main concern.

Three points require final emphasis:

1   I hope this chapter has highlighted the difficult intellectual debates practitioners must grapple with whilst undertaking the work of making sense of autism in an inclusive context. It should be abundantly clear that it is not easy being an inclusive practitioner supporting clients with autism. This will become clearer in the ensuing chapters.

2   I hope that I have managed to argue convincingly that practitioner knowledge and understanding of autism is a vital grounding for effective practice. It is only via the 'autism lens' – a sound knowledge and understanding of the condition – that practitioners can gain an accurate insight into the surface behaviours and responses of clients with autism, and then assess, plan, evaluate and adapt the environment for inclusion. The argument that this is exclusionary or discriminatory is difficult to uphold when one is confronted by the body of research, referenced above, highlighting the consequences, for clients, of a lack of practitioner training. Persistently high exclusion statistics further evidence this, with one in five children with autism being excluded from school at least once in their school life (Reid & Batten 2007) and high levels of exclusion of children and adults across health and social care services (Scottish Government 2008).

3   Though autism and inclusion are both highly complex and perhaps conflicted fields, I hope it is possible to see that the debates around them are not intractable. Whilst there will never be easy and unequivocal answers to the theoretical controversies and dilemmas presented in this chapter and chapter 1, I suggest that greater synthesis can be achieved by seeking out commonalities and striving for balanced, holistic, person-centred solutions.

The 'integrative position' arguably provides a fruitful starting point in this collaborative endeavour. It is now vital for the future development of service provision that the essentially healthy aspiration to uncover how inclusion might best work is achieved in a more negotiatory fashion that puts people with autism first and ideology second.

In the next chapter, the focus remains on the analysis of the factors that influence good autism practice. However, the emphasis shifts slightly from a preoccupation with theoretical concerns, though these will continue to be relevant, to how policy and theory are translated into practice. The specific interest of chapter 3 is therefore implementation and how practitioners in different service contexts *enable* inclusion and the development of individual potential. We will also examine the barriers that subvert good practice and limit successful outcomes.

References

Aitken, K. (2008) Keynote presentation at 'Partners in Autism' Conference, Dundee, September 2008.

Allan, J. (2008)*Rethinking Inclusion: The Philosophers of Difference in Practice*, Dordrecht: Springer.

Autism Act (2009) London: The Stationery Office. Accessible: http://www.legislation. gov.uk/ukpga/2009/15/pdfs/ukpga_20090015_en.pdf (accessed July 2014).

Batten, A., Corbett, C., Rosenblatt, M., Withers, L.T. & Yuille, R. (2006) *Make School Make Sense – Autism & Education: The Reality for Families Today*, London: National Autistic Society.

Batten, A. & Daly, J. (2006) *Make School Make Sense: Autism and Education in Scotland – The Reality for Families*, London: National Autistic Society. Accessible: bera.ac.uk/publications (accessed May 2008).

Baron-Cohen, S. (2000) Is Asperger Syndrome/High Functioning Autism necessarily a disability? *Development and Psychopathology*, 12, 489–500.

Baron-Cohen, S. (2003) *The Essential Difference: The Truth about the Male and Female Brain*, New York: Basic Books.

Boucher, J. (2009) *The Autistic Spectrum: Characteristics, Causes and Practical Issues*, London: Sage.

Broderick, A.A. & Ne'eman, A. (2008) Autism as metaphor: narrative and counternarrative, *International Journal of Inclusive Education*, 12/5, 459–476.

Carlberg, C. & Kavale, K. (1980) The efficacy of special versus regular class placement for exceptional children: a meta-analysis, *Journal of Special Education*, 14, 295–309.

Cigman, R. (ed.) (2007) Editorial introduction, in *Included or Excluded? The Challenge of the Mainstream for Some SEN Children*, xv–xxviii, London: Routledge.

Cook, B.G. & Schirmer, B.R. (2003) What is special about special education? Overview and analysis. *Journal of Special Education*, 37/3, 200–204.

Davis, P. & Florian, L. (2004) *Teaching Strategies and Approaches for Pupils with Special Educational Needs: A Scoping Study* (Research Report no. 516), London: DfES. Accessible: http://dera.ioe.ac.uk/id/eprint/6059 (accessed July 2014).

Department of Children, Schools & Families (DCSF) (2009) *Inclusion Development Programme: Supporting Pupils on the Autism Spectrum*, Nottingham: DCSF.

Department of Health (DoH) (2006) *Better Services for People with an Autistic Spectrum Disorder: A Note Clarifying Current Government Policy and Describing Good Practice*, London: DoH.

Dunlop, A.-W., Tait, C. & Robinson, A. (2009) *Policy into Practice: Accreditation Project Report. A Collaborative Autism Education and Training Project*, NCAS and Scottish Society for Autism, Glasgow: University of Strathclyde.

Dyson, D. (2005) Special education as the way to equity: an alternative approach? In J. Rix, K. Simmons, M. Nind & K. Sheehy (eds), *Policy and Power in Inclusive Education*, London: Routledge.

Florian, L. (ed.) (2007) Reimagining special education, in *The Sage Handbook of Special Education*, 7–20. London: Sage.

Frith, U. (1991) *Autism and Asperger Syndrome*, Cambridge: Cambridge University Press.

Gillman, M., Heyman, B. & Swain, J. (2000) What's in a name? The implications of diagnosis for people with learning difficulties and their family carers, *Disability and Society*, 15, 389–409.

Goodley, D. & Runswick-Cole, K. (2011) Problematising policy: conceptions of 'child', 'disabled' and 'parents' in social policy in England, *International Journal of Inclusive Education*, 15/1, 71–85.

Graham, L. (2006) Caught in the net: a Foucaultian interrogation of the incidental effects of limited notions of inclusion, *International Journal of Inclusive Education*, 10/1, 3–25.

Griffiths, M. (ed.) (2003) *Action for Social Justice in Education: Fairly Different*, Maidenhead: Open University Press.

HMIE (HM Inspectorate of Education) (2006) *Education for Pupils with Autism Spectrum Disorders*, Livingston: HMIE.

Ho, A. (2004) To be labelled, or not to be labelled: that is the question, *British Journal of Learning Disabilities*, 32, 86–92.

Humphrey, N. & Lewis, S. (2008) What does inclusion mean for pupils on the autistic spectrum in mainstream secondary schools? *Journal of Research in Special Educational Needs*, 8/3, 132–140.

Jones, G., English, A., Guldberg, K., Jordan, R., Richardson, P. & Waltz, M. (2008) Educational provision for children and young people on the autism spectrum living in England: a review of current practice, issues and challenges. Accessible: http://www.autismeducationtrust.org.uk/resources/research.aspx (accessed March 2014).

Jordan, R. (2005) Autistic spectrum disorders, in B. Norwich (ed.), *Special Teaching for Special Children? Pedagogy for Special Educational Needs*, 110–123, Milton Keynes: Open University Press.

Jordan, R. (2006) *Autism Spectrum Disorder (ASD) or Autism Spectrum Condition (ASC)?* Cape Town: World Autism Congress, South Africa.

Lawson, W. (2008) *Concepts of Normality: The Autistic and Typical Spectrum*, London: Jessica Kingsley.

Lewis, A. & Norwich, B. (eds) (2005) *Special Teaching for Special Children? Pedagogies for Inclusion*, Maidenhead: Open University Press.

MacKay, T.A.W.N. & Dunlop, A.W.A. (2004) *The Development of a National Training Framework for Autistic Spectrum Disorders, A Study of Training for Professionals Working in the Field of ASD in Scotland*, Glasgow: National Autistic Society & University of Strathclyde.

Molloy, H. & Vasil, L. (2004) *Asperger Syndrome, Adolescence and Identity*, London: Jessica Kingsley.

NAS (National Autistic Society) (2007) *Autism & Independence: A Guide for Local Authorities*, London: NAS.

NAS (National Autistic Society) (2014) Statistics accessible: http://www.autism.org. uk/about-autism/myths-facts-and-statistics/some-facts-and-statistics.aspx (accessed July 2014).

Norwich, B. (2007) *Dilemmas of Difference, Inclusion and Disability: International Perspectives and Future Directions*, London: Routledge.

Parry, J., Rix, J., Kumrai, R. & Walsh, C. (2010) Introduction: Another place, in J. Rix, M. Nind, K. Sheehy, K. Simmons, J. Parry & R. Kumrai (eds), *Equality, Participation and Inclusion: Diverse Contexts*, 1–8, London: David Fulton.

Public Health Institute of Scotland (PHIS) (2001) *Autistic Spectrum Disorders: Needs Assessment Report*. Available: http://www.scotland.gov.uk/Resource/ Doc/1095/0076895.pdf (accessed July 2014).

Reid, B. & Batten, A. (2007) *Make School Make Sense for Me: Children & Young People with Autism Speak Out*, London: National Autistic Society.

Schreibman, L. (2005) *The Science and Fiction of Autism*, London: Harvard University Press.

Scottish Government (2008) *Commissioning Services for People on the Autism Spectrum: Policy and Practice Guidance*, Edinburgh: Scottish Government. Accessible: www.scotland.gov.uk (accessed April 2009).

Scottish Government (2011) *The Scottish Strategy for Autism: Overview*, Edinburgh: Scottish Government.

SIGN (Scottish Intercollegiate Guidelines Network) (2007) *Assessment, Diagnosis and Clinical Interventions for Children and Young People with Autism Spectrum Disorders: A National Clinical Approach*, NHS Scotland. Accessible: www. sign.ac.uk (accessed March 2009).

Thomas, G. & Loxley, A. (2007) *Deconstructing Special Education and Constructing Inclusion*, 2nd edition, Maidenhead: Open University Press.

Williams, J. (2014) Private correspondence.

Chapter 3

Theory into practice
Enabling participation

In chapter 2, it was argued that practitioner training in autism awareness is a vital underpinning of effective service provision in inclusive contexts. It was repeatedly stressed that a sound understanding of the condition, and a firm grasp of the main theories of autism, were absolutely pivotal to the endeavour of making sense of the surface behaviour and responses of clients with autism in any workplace context. At the same time, the complexities of using this 'autism lens' were squarely acknowledged and explored, especially as they interact with dilemmas associated with inclusive practice.

The next step is to explore how, exactly, practitioners apply the autism lens to identify individual needs, pinpoint priority targets, and select and plan effective approaches and interventions to enable participation and learning. In other words, how do practitioners transform theory into practice? This will involve critical discussion of the following key themes:

- Individualisation and assessment
- Approaches and interventions

Each of these themes will be explored in relation to current literature and research in order to establish an evidence base for good practice in autism. A case study will then be provided that explores how these elements are enacted in a specific service setting.

Individualisation and assessment

Individualisation and assessment go hand in hand. Together they are imperative for the conceptualisation and development of appropriate and well-focused support.

Individualisation refers to the process of modification that is necessary to meet the distinctive strengths and needs of a particular child, young person or adult with autism (Barton et al. 2011). Of course, individualisation is a feature of good inclusive practice for all clients in any service context, since everyone has individual needs of some sort or another that must be taken into account. However, the importance of individualisation is amplified in relation to individuals with autism for two reasons. Firstly, high-functioning individuals with autism and those with a diagnosis of Asperger's Syndrome are especially vulnerable to being treated as neurotypical, i.e. as though they do *not* have autism. The reasons for this were explored in chapter 2 and relate, largely, to a lack of autism awareness amongst service practitioners. In such circumstances, a client's autism-specific needs may be completely overlooked, leading to a failure of support and, in many instances, the breakdown of the service placement. The second reason stems from the opposite impulse, i.e. the tendency to over-generalise and to make assumptions about the needs of individuals with autism on the basis of their diagnosis alone, rather than on the basis of an analysis of the behavioural characteristics of the individual. Again, this was discussed in chapter 2 in relation to concerns about the dangers of medical labelling. People with autism are not a homogenous group – far from it. Though all individuals diagnosed with the condition experience challenges in relation to social communication, social understanding and flexibility of thinking and behaviour, autism is a spectrum condition that affects people in different ways and to different degrees. Individualisation therefore essentially entails getting to know clients as individuals with autism, rather than as autistic individuals – a subtle but essential distinction.

Assessment informed by a knowledge and understanding of autism is the main way of achieving accurate individualisation. Assessment refers to deliberative actions undertaken by practitioners to gather information and feedback from a variety of sources in order to create or modify a package of support (Black & Wiliam 1998). Of course, the focus of information gathering will depend entirely on the purpose of the assessment. This focus might be directly related to autism, e.g. the behavioural characteristics of autism for a diagnostic assessment, or it may be more general, e.g. personal care needs for a social care assessment, or learning needs for an educational assessment. Irrespective of the focus, if a client has a diagnosis of autism, several important considerations immediately arise:

- Assessment data should be drawn from a range of environments since people with autism can function very differently from one context to another
- The assessment process must be collaborative and involve, wherever possible, the individual with autism, their parents/carers and other professionals involved in their support so that the emerging profile is holistic and meaningful to all
- The assessment itself must be autism specific (see box 3.1) or sensitively adapted to meet the needs of clients with autism
- It must be administered by a practitioner with autism training
- It must assess strengths as well as challenges

(Ravet 2013)

Box 3.1 Examples of autism-specific assessments

Screening assessments

The Modified Checklist for Autism in Toddlers (M-CHAT)

Diagnostic assessments

The Diagnostic Interview for Social and Communication Disorders (DISCO)
(Wing et al. 2002)
Autism Spectrum Rating Scales (ASRS) (Goldstein & Naglieri 2010)
Autistic Diagnostic Interview – Revised (ADI-R) (Lord et. al. 1994)
Autism Disorder Observation Schedule (ADOS) (Lord et al. 1989)
Child Autism Rating Scale (CARS) (Schopler et al. 1980)
Gilliam Autism Rating Scale 2 (GARS-2) (Gilliam 2005)
Gilliam Asperger's Diagnostic Scale (GADS) (Gilliam 2001)
ASD: Diagnostic Adult (Matson et al. 2007)

General assessments

Communication of Thinking Skills Assessment Record (Silver 2005)
The Autistic Continuum: an assessment and intervention schedule for
investigating behaviours, skills and needs of children with autism (Aarons &
Gittens 1992)
The Sensory Checklist (Biel & Peske 2005)
Children's Communication Checklist (CCC) (Bishop 2003)
Psychoeducational Profile – Revised (PEP-R) (Schopler et al. 2004)
Adolescent and Adult Psychoeducational Profile (AAPEP) (Mesibov et al. 1989)

Where these conditions are met, the data yielded by assessment is more likely to be well focused and accurate. It will enable practitioners to identify priority targets and build individualised packages of support that address identified needs and capitalise on identified strengths.

However, research indicates that individualisation and assessment in relation to autism is problematic across service contexts. For example, in some health care settings in the UK, client access to both 'diagnostic assessment' and to an 'assessment of needs' is erratic (PHIS 2001, Scottish Executive 2006, Daly 2008, Rosenblatt 2008). A 'diagnostic assessment' is a formal procedure carried out by a medical professional to establish whether an individual meets the criteria for a diagnosis of autism. It identifies the specific manifestations of the condition and establishes levels of severity across the triad of impairments. An 'assessment of needs' is a formal assessment process led by a social worker to identify a client's community care needs following diagnosis; for example, their need for personal care and support for toileting, washing, dressing, shopping, etc. This assessment is used as a basis for referral to community care services for individuals who face complex challenges. The diagnostic assessment and the assessment of needs generally go hand in hand so that the former triggers the latter. An assessment of needs is then periodically updated as client needs and circumstances evolve.

However, in a study of 151 adults with autism in Scotland (Daly 2008), 52% of the adults with autism and 62% of the adults with Asperger's Syndrome indicated that they had not had an assessment of needs since the age of 18 because they either did not have a social worker, or they did not have a social worker with sufficient understanding of autism to undertake the assessment. This finding was linked to the fact that 56% of the cohort had found it difficult to access a basic diagnostic assessment, without which it is invariably more difficult to secure assessment entitlements and attract appropriate support. Interestingly, these perceptions were confirmed by 69% of the Community Health Partnerships (CHPs) involved in the research. These professionals acknowledged the dearth of diagnostic services for autism and linked this directly to a lack of training, time and money.

These findings are sobering and serve to remind us that the needs of people with autism are often invisible to the very health professionals they turn to for help. The implications of this are deeply troubling. For example, if autism is undiagnosed and the characteristic features of the condition are not picked up, mental health practitioners may overlook causes of distress linked to autism, fail to appropriately individualise psychological interventions such as cognitive behavioural therapies (Crabtree et al. 2011) and may prescribe treatments that are 'contra-indicatory' (ibid.), e.g. neuroleptic medication to which individuals with autism can be sensitive (Woodbury-Smith & Volkmar 2009). However, recent NHS guidance (e.g. SIGN 2007/2012, NICE 2011, DoH 2010) explicitly highlights the problem of lack of training and the 'inequalities in healthcare and service provision' that result (NICE 2011, p. 5). The NICE guidance sets out to address the problem by providing comprehensive, evidence-based recommendations for assessment and clinical intervention for services throughout the UK. The Department of Health (2010) guidance provides autism training recommendations for all NHS practitioners, including GPs. These recommendations are supported by autism legislation in England and Northern Ireland so health authorities have a duty to follow them. In Scotland and Wales, equivalent guidance falls within the recommendations of national autism strategies. Health practitioners are under no statutory obligation to follow the guidance since these strategies lack legislative force. The impact of their recommendations therefore remains to be seen.

Unfortunately, assessment in educational contexts is no less problematic. Research indicates that in many educational settings in Europe and the UK it has not yet become widely appreciated that inclusive teaching should be informed by inclusive assessment; indeed, there is little research, policy or guidance available to teachers in this area (EADSNE 2009, Jones et al 2009, DCSF 2010, Wilkinson & Twist 2010). In schools, assessment for children and young people with autism is rarely autism specific or sufficiently adapted to accommodate individual learner needs (Wilkinson & Twist 2010). It is simply assumed that the range of assessment tools currently available will somehow work for all learners. Research indicates that this is linked to the underlying problem of inadequate professional development in autism and also poor leadership, lack of time, negative attitudes toward autism and inclusion, and a narrow interpretation of inclusion and inclusive practice (Humphrey & Lewis 2008, Ravet 2011, Ravet 2013). This means that learners with autism may be exposed to assessment processes that are exclusionary, stressful, and generate partial and inaccurate feedback. In these cases, the assessment process itself becomes a major barrier to inclusion, causing profound problems down the line as unreliable data is used, often unknowingly, as a basis for the development of future support.

For example, if teachers do not understand autism, they are unlikely to appreciate that students facing summative assessments, such as national examinations, may need accommodations to the administration of the assessment as well as adaptations to content. This is far from uncommon (HMIE 2006, DCSF 2010) and therefore represents a considerable injustice. It is not difficult to imagine the stress it generates for pupils with autism and the implications it could have for their learning development, progress and future prospects.

Equally, teachers lacking autism awareness may fail to appreciate how ongoing formative assessment in the classroom might be disadvantageous to learners with autism. Formative assessment refers to the ongoing use of observation, questioning and dialogue with pupils, as well as learner self-assessment and peer assessment, which enables teachers to establish how learners are progressing and plan their teaching accordingly (Black & Wiliam 1998). These assessment activities tend to be heavily 'talk' based and therefore assume a capacity for effective social interaction, social communication and flexibility of thought on the part of the learner. Clearly, by definition, these are areas of difficulty for learners with autism. The self-assessment element can be particularly challenging, as individuals with autism frequently lack a strong sense of self linked to poor theory of mind, and have difficulties with introspection and reflexivity (Happe 2003). Indeed, the literature indicates that this particular aspect of formative assessment is an 'area of concern' (EADSNE 2009) and has led to calls for 'clearer guidance and focused teacher training' in both autism and the assessment of this group (Wilkinson & Twist 2010).

Formative assessment must therefore be sensitively adapted to reduce reliance on dialogue and questioning and to support self-reflection. Using visual structuring is vital here for it reduces reliance on verbal communication, thereby reducing anxiety and enabling participation. Formative assessment based on visual structuring is more likely to generate focused, accurate, learner-centred assessment data. The importance of visual structuring is discussed in more detail below.

Effective assessment is therefore a crucial starting point for intervention. It enables practitioners to gather data about a client's specific needs as a basis for the construction of individualised support packages. It also has a vital secondary function since it provides base-line data that can be used to compare future outcomes and enable evaluation of practice effectiveness. Future inputs can then be progressively adapted to ensure progress towards successful outcomes.

In summary, three important points have been made:

1   Individualisation and assessment are inextricably linked
2   Assessment must make use of autism-specific assessment tools or tools that have been modified to ensure that they are inclusive and accurate
3   Assessment that is not modified distorts support and renders inclusion meaningless

It is therefore axiomatic that effective assessment must be informed by an understanding of autism. But having achieved this, what next? What interventions might be developed and what evidence do we have that they work?

Autism interventions: the evidence base

There is now a plethora of interventions that help people with autism to participate and fulfil their potential at home, school, at work and in the community. These include:

- **Behavioural and developmental interventions** e.g. Applied Behaviour Analysis (ABA), Early Start Denver Model, Pivotal Response Treatment (PRT)
- **Educational interventions** e.g. Treatment and Education of Autistic and Communication-Handicapped Children (TEACCH), Social Communication/Emotional Regulation/Transactional Support (SCERTS), Social Stories, Floortime, Higashi Method, SPELL Framework
- **Therapeutic interventions** e.g. Nordoff Robbins Music Therapy, Intensive Interaction, Self-Regulation Programme Of Awareness & Resilience in Kids (SPARKS)
- **Interventions to support communication** e.g. Picture Exchange Communication System (PECS), Augmentative and Alternative Communication (AAC) devices and methods
- **Motor and sensory interventions** e.g. sensory integrative therapy, physiotherapy
- **Pharmaceutical interventions** e.g. risperidone (for hyperactivity), melatonin (for sleep disorders)

Clearly this is good news, as they offer hope to the autism community and provide a range of options to meet the needs of a highly diverse population. However, there is currently no intervention that has been scientifically proven to be effective for all individuals with autism, and few that, on their own, have been proven to produce substantial benefits. A minority may even be harmful (Francis 2005). One might therefore conclude that the evidence base for autism interventions is generally weak. However, let us look at this conclusion more closely.

The term 'scientifically proven' refers only to research that involves randomised control trials (RCTs), i.e. large-scale studies in which participants are randomly allocated either to the intervention group or to a control group that does not receive the target intervention. The random allocation ensures that participants and those around them do not know they are involved and therefore do not change their behaviour or invest in a positive outcome. The idea of the control is that it makes it easier to establish whether or not changes in performance can be attributed directly to the intervention itself. A key reason for the seemingly weak scientific evidence base mentioned above is the fact that few intervention studies are actually funded and conducted (Mills & Marchant 2011) since the majority of funding has, until relatively recently, gone straight to research on causation and diagnosis (McGregor et al. 2008). Another problem is that many of the studies that have been conducted do not meet high-quality standards in terms of their design, sampling and methods (Francis 2005). Some of the key concerns are as follows:

- Lack of independent studies, i.e. conducted by researchers with no vested interest
- Many RCT studies are based on IQ tests – due to poor administration these are often unreliable for individuals with ASC
- Few studies are 'blind', i.e. participants and those around them know they are involved, which can influence results
- No 'control' or comparison group – it is therefore difficult to attribute changes to the intervention itself
- Poor documentation of intervention procedures, therefore no reliable data with which to evaluate and replicate studies
- Poor record of severity of impairment – thus to whom do the results apply?
- Small sample sizes

(Humphrey & Parkinson 2006, pp. 79–80)

Some researchers therefore argue that we need more funding for scientific intervention research so that we can establish a more convincing evidence base (Francis 2005). This is important to enable people with autism, families and professionals to ascertain which interventions are trustworthy and which might be effective for a particular individual.

However, some researchers question the notion that studies based on RCTs are the only 'gold star' approach to autism research. They challenge the idea that RCTs can tell us everything we need to know. For example, Mesibov and Shea (2010) argue that few practitioners actually use single interventions or adopt them in a pure form. Rather, they take a 'personalised approach' by drawing on a variety of interventions depending on the client's needs and specific characteristics (ibid.). They argue that what matters in this sort of research is how well interventions work together for a particular individual or group, in a particular context, at a particular time, and propose that the study of these more complex situations calls for small-scale, person-centred, qualitative research methods that can provide detailed, in-depth evidence of efficacy. Arguably, this form of research is equally legitimate providing, of course, that it meets high methodological standards within its own paradigm. Indeed, Mesibov and Shea argue that this research can yield feedback about the trustworthiness and validity of interventions that is just as useful to the autism community.

It might therefore be argued that the apparent weakness of the evidence base for autism interventions arises, in part, from the overly narrow and restrictive emphasis on RCTs (Mills & Marchant 2011). This emphasis has arisen because autism research has its early roots in medical research and the theoretical perspectives associated with the quantitative scientific paradigm. However, there is now a growing volume of applied research issuing from psychology, education, speech and language therapy and other such disciplines, which operates within different theoretical perspectives and draws on a range of different research approaches. McGregor et al. (2008) contend that these different approaches need not vie with each other for superiority, as this simply leads to division, fragmentation and confusion. Rather, greater integration of perspectives is increasingly necessary in order to reach a fuller and more coherent understanding of how autism is addressed in different contexts. Thus, it is in our common interests to build up a broader, richer, more varied and integrated evidence base that includes a range of high-quality qualitative *and* quantitative research that can tell us as much as possible about the efficacy of different interventions and the relationships between them. Indeed, some claim that this is a vital next step in the evolution of autism research (Leekham & McGregor 2008).

Autism interventions: the SPELL framework

It is not within the limits of this book to explore the various interventions available to the autism community and to the professionals who support them. Instead, we will deepen our discussion by exploring the SPELL framework in detail. SPELL (NAS 2014) is an example of a person-centred framework that combines a range of interventions depending on individual needs. This framework is used widely in education, therapeutic and social care contexts, by parents in the home and by individuals with autism. It therefore has broad relevance and has proven useful and effective.

SPELL has been the intervention framework recommended by the National Autistic Society (NAS) since 1964 and stands for Structure, Positive approaches and expectations, Empathy, Low arousal and Links (Mills 2013). The framework is based on cognitive learning theory and is therefore concerned with how people think, understand and know, and how best to structure and organise learning and the learning environment so that cognitive processing works as efficiently and effectively as possible. The five principles of SPELL clearly reflect these concerns. We will begin by exploring its principles, its evidence base, and why, in terms of the triad of impairments, it is considered to meet the needs of clients with autism. We will then see how the SPELL framework is implemented in practice in a case study.

S for Structure

> The term structure in autism interventions generally describes organisa-
> tion of time, space and sequences of events within the learning environ-
> ment in order to make learning activities clearer and easier to perform.
>
> (Mesibov & Shea 2010, p. 572)

There is a wide consensus amongst researchers that structured learning, incorporating a high level of visual structure, is one of the most important and effective interventions for individuals with ASC. It is reported to improve communication, social skills, behaviour, independent functioning and self-help skills (Schopler et al. 1995, Ozonoff & Cathcart 1998, Siasperas & Beadle-Brown 2006, Mesibov & Shea 2010, Mills & Marchant 2011).

Individuals with autism benefit from additional visual structure largely because they have difficulty ordering and organising information and making sense of verbal communication. Our current understanding of autism links these difficulties to underlying weaknesses of executive control, central coherence and theory of mind as explained in chapter 2. Visual structure helps by removing reliance on verbal input, as well as dependence on the constant gestural and physical prompting of others that can lead to dependence and learned helplessness. It therefore replaces mediating figures, significantly reduces the incoming cognitive traffic constantly issuing from busy hospital waiting rooms, therapy units, respite settings and other service environments and enables learners to gain predictability, control and autonomy.

Visual structure supports order and organisation by explicitly focusing attention on 'time, space and sequences of events' (Mesibov & Shea 2010), representing them in a form that can be quickly, easily and directly assimilated using, as appropriate, concrete objects, photographs, pictures, line drawings, symbols and/or written words (see box 3.2). The approach clearly capitalises on the tendency of individuals with autism to show superior visual processing (Dakin & Frith 2005).

Box 3.2: Visual supports

I think in pictures. Words are like a second language to me...when somebody speaks to me, his words are instantly translated into pictures... One of the most profound mysteries of autism has been the remarkable ability of most autistic people to excel at visual spatial skills while performing so poorly at verbal skills.

(Grandin 1995, p. 19)

Types of visual support

- Objects of reference, e.g. plate to represent dinner time
- Photographs
- Miniatures of real objects
- Coloured pictures
- Line drawings
- Written words

Some examples of line drawings

Visual safety instructions

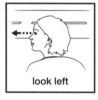 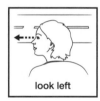

look left   look right   look left   cross the road

Look left–right–left before crossing the street

Visual hand-washing sequence

turn on water   soap   wash hands   turn off water   dry hands

Visual rules

No biting!

Visual task schedule

Bedtime

	Sunday	Monday	Tuesday	Wednesday	Thursday	Friday	Saturday
take off clothes	✓						
bath	✓						
put on pyjamas	✓						
brush teeth	✓						
read	✓						
bed	✓						

However, the importance of structuring goes beyond the provision of visual structure and involves the re-organisation of workplaces and spaces, and the explicit clarification of their purposes and the social expectations associated with them. Thus, structuring implies consideration of the organisation of the physical and sensory environment, the learning environment, the communication environment and the social environment, as these are elements of any context that can cause considerable confusion for people with autism – especially when they are new to the context.

This high degree of structuring is necessary because change, as we know, can be very challenging where there is inflexibility of thought and behaviour. Problems with social understanding mean that individuals with autism find it difficult to anticipate the purposes of new contexts, and to identify and apply the social rules and conventions associated with them. They therefore run the risk of contravening the rules, attracting negative feedback and experiencing stress and humiliation. Further, problems with social communication mean that they cannot simply turn to others for clear explanations of how things work and how they should behave, as lengthy verbal explanations may simply cause more, rather than less, confusion and anxiety. It is little wonder, given these multiple difficulties, that many individuals with autism become anxious on entering new contexts, and readily flee from them when things go wrong. Clearly some structuring of the environment is essential to ease access and enable navigation around the many different service contexts that people with autism must inevitably encounter. The function of structure is therefore to bring order where there is chaos, and to create the conditions for safe, calm participation.

Structure can be achieved on a number of levels, in a number of different ways, by drawing on a range of techniques and interventions as indicated below:

a) Structuring the physical/sensory environment

- Provide a workstation/quiet table for focused tasks to reduce distractions
- Carefully consider who is seated next to/around the individual to ensure a supportive and empathetic peer group
- Try to create a low-arousal sensory environment to avoid sensory overwhelm (e.g. remove clutter and known sensory triggers, keep walls clear, keep colour/lighting/noise levels low, avoid strong smells)
- Capitalise on sensory preferences and channel these constructively/use them as rewards
- Consider safety: remove sharp items, cover switches, use safety glass in windows, etc.
- Label areas/resources/seating to provide predictability and to facilitate autonomy
- Colour code and symbolise buildings to ease accessibility

b) Structure the learning environment

- Create visual organisation to enhance predictability, control and independence, e.g. provide visual timetables, visual learning plans, visual task schedules, visual rules, etc. (see examples box 3.2)
- Organise tasks physically using left–right routines, in/out trays, etc. and ensure consistency
- Use visual prompts to facilitate independence and *fade* verbal, physical and gestural prompts that create dependence
- Start tasks with a visual review using mind mapping to support transfer of knowledge and skills
- Present intentions/goals (what is to be done) and success criteria (how we will know) visually to provide clarity and to promote understanding and independence
- Structure participation in group work by phasing it in slowly, keeping it short and clarifying roles and rules visually
- Structure activity/task sheets – make them uncluttered, unambiguous, short and succinct
- Use concrete/visual supports to assist understanding of abstract concepts, e.g. by using objects, models, photographs, DVDs, etc.
- Enable participation and challenge passivity by providing opportunities to plan, choose, comment, question, evaluate. Make these visual and concrete, e.g. use smiley scales, traffic lights, comment boxes, 'choose boards' with visual choices, etc.
- Provide visual opportunities for self–assessment and peer assessment, e.g. thumbs-up/down, visual rating scales, etc.
- Allow frequent breaks to avoid overwhelm and stress
- Be flexible: people can learn with a hat on, shoes off, and whilst speaking in an American accent!
- Motivate! Capitalise on special interests/reward appropriate responses

c) Structure the communication environment

- Wherever possible, lower verbalisations and use visuals to support communication and understanding
- Avoid ambiguous language such as idioms and metaphors which can be taken literally and cause confusion
- Use the individual's name to cue communication and to establish joint focus
- Keep verbal instructions short, unambiguous and clear or they will be tuned out
- Teach communication skills, e.g. scripting, PECS, sign language, Makaton, talking mats, etc. (see examples, box 3.3)

Box 3.3: Teaching skills visually

PECS: stands for Picture Exchange Communication System. This system is based on the idea that children who can't talk can be taught to initiate interaction and communicate their needs using pictures. The individual exchanges a picture for an item they want.

Sign language: this is a system of communication using visual gestures and signs, as used by deaf people.

Makaton: Makaton is a language programme that uses a combination of physical and hand gestures, facial expressions and spoken language to support communication.

Talking mats: these are mats to which pictures are attached and used in an interactive way to visually explore issues and record thoughts. Talking mats require three sets of symbols – topics, options and a visual scale – and a space on which to display them. The mats may be physical or digital.

Social Stories: these are a way of explaining social situations, rules and expectations visually. They involve using a narrative structure to explain the social issue in a simple, clear and structured way. The Social Story can be written in words or in a comic strip cartoon format.

Scripting: scripting involves providing short conversation sequences that are written down, memorised and utilised by individuals with autism, e.g. a sequence on how to greet people in the street: 'Good morning, how are you?' They are usually laminated and carried around with the individual so that they can be used as visual prompts in real social situations. As the script is practised and perfected, it can slowly be reduced to a one-word prompt and then faded when it is no longer needed.

Video modelling: video modelling involves the use of video recordings to provide a visual model of a targeted behaviour or skill. This takes the form of a recording of an actor or some other stand-in engaging in the target behaviour or skill that is then reviewed and practised by the learner. Alternatively, it might involve self-modelling, review and analysis, or a combination of both.

---

d) Structure the social environment

- Explicitly identify, explain and routinise social conventions, e.g. entry and exit routines, social greetings, etc. (provide visual supports)
- Explicitly identify, explain and routinise social rules and expectations, e.g. take coat off, queue here, etc. (provide visual supports)

- Explain how rules apply in different contexts to support transfer, e.g. use social stories (see box 3.3)
- Foster peer support to avoid marginalisation and isolation, e.g. via buddy schemes and other peer support networks, e.g. Circle of Friends
- Provide clear routines and structure for unstructured times to avoid confusion and stress, e.g. hospital waiting room, school playtime
- Use visual approaches to support the development of social skills, e.g. via video modelling (see box 3.3)
- Highlight and praise/reward appropriate, positive behaviour/responses so that individuals know when they are 'getting it right'

P for Positive approaches and expectations

Taking a positive approach to autism means not taking the path of least resistance by habitually doing things for or to people, and avoiding the assumption that people with autism have fixed abilities or limited potential. It is therefore about positive attitudes and beliefs. It means:

- Maintaining high expectations
- Being person-centred
- Being inclusive
- Supporting acquisition of new knowledge, understanding and skills (see above)
- Facilitating choice and valuing contributions
- Capitalising on strengths
- Using special interests positively to motivate and reward
- Using positive behaviour support and understanding that much reactive behaviour is stress, not defiance
- Avoiding labelling and, instead, use positive language
- Creating an environment that enables participation, independence and the fulfilment of potential

The notion of Person-Centred Active Support (Ashman & Beadle-Brown 2006) is applied in community care contexts (though, arguably, it is relevant in any service context). It incorporates many of the elements above in an attempt to enhance provision for individuals with support needs, including clients with autism. The aim is to increase client levels of active engagement in social, leisure, recreational and practical activities in the home or community by improving the quality of support provided by community care staff.

This initiative follows concerns that clients with learning disabilities in community care establishments are actively engaged in social and leisure activities for only 11% of the day, whilst non-disabled people are engaged for 90% of the day (ibid.). There is evidence that positive, person-centred support that draws on the approaches listed above is key to increasing participation, enhancing skills and adaptive behaviour, and improving general quality of life (Ashman & Beadle-Brown 2006, Stancliffe et al. 2007, Beadle-Brown et al. 2012).

E for Empathy

Studies in educational contexts indicate that the personal qualities of individual staff are highly significant in establishing the relationships and trust that underpin successful outcomes for individuals with autism (Peeters & Jordan 1999). It has been found, for example, that school staff need a range of specific qualities such as the capacity to act 'counter-intuitively', think flexibly and unconventionally, be tolerant, adaptable and resourceful, take risks, be resilient, show emotional intelligence and be perceptive and empathetic (Ashton Smith 2011). It is not unreasonable to assume that the same qualities would be required in other service contexts.

The quality of empathy is possibly the most important quality of all – hence its emphasis within the SPELL framework. Empathy is the capacity to understand and imaginatively enter into another's situation, feelings and motives. According to Goleman (2007) it has three dimensions. 'Cognitive empathy', in the context of good autism practice, is insight into the thoughts and feelings of others that draws on a bedrock of theoretical knowledge and understanding of autism. 'Emotional empathy' enables one to tune in to the client's emotional experience and to feel alongside them. It draws on self-knowledge and understanding of one's own emotions. Finally, 'compassionate empathy' is aroused by a deeply felt concern that provides the impetus to do something – to feel 'moved to help' (ibid., p. 2). All three aspects of empathy are necessary to imbue autism theory with human meaning and to ensure effective support for clients with autism.

- Cognitive empathy: try to understand how the autistic pupil thinks, communicates, learns and experiences the world (use the autism lens!)
- Emotional empathy: be self-aware (notice your own beliefs, assumptions and feelings) and consider how they may influence, and possibly distort, your understanding of learner behaviour. Try to remain calm when the learner is stressed, as aversive reactions tend to lead to escalation
- Compassionate empathy: think about what you can change in yourself and in the environment, not how to 'fix' the learner

If a member of staff shows a consistently weak capacity for empathy, all the autism training in the world will have little impact on them as it cannot be translated into deep personal understanding and authentic caring. This clearly has implications for staff recruitment, deployment and retention since staff who are well suited to supporting clients with autism are much more likely to be effective and find the work personally and professionally fulfilling. On the other hand, staff ill suited to it are more likely to be overwhelmed by the 'otherness' of clients and the complexity of the demands placed on them, and will burn out quickly. Attracting the right staff and matching staff carefully to clients is therefore an important consideration in any service context.

L for Low arousal

In chapter 2 we noted that many individuals with autism can be highly discomfited by certain stimuli in the environment to which they are especially sensitive (Marco et al. 2011). For example, sounds in the environment that most of us can integrate and ignore, like the low hum of a computer on standby or a sudden outburst of shouting or crying, can be overwhelming and saturating to people with aural hypersensitivity. Likewise, the texture of seating or carpets, the visual impact of colourful posters or brightly painted walls, the smell of perfume or detergents, or the taste of particular foods and drinks can all be a source of agitation and, in some cases, a trigger for upset and challenging behaviour.

To add to this, we have discussed how difficult social communication and interaction can be for people with autism. If they are constantly confronted by requirements to pay attention, look, listen, react and respond, it should not be surprising that they will soon find this extremely tiring and seek to withdraw from the clamour of constant demands from other people (ibid.).

For both of these reasons it is important that the service environment for clients with autism is low arousal, i.e. especially designed and organised to minimise sensory stimulation and ensure order and calm. The following measures can be helpful:

- Talk less! Use visual supports much more!
- Also fade physical and gestural prompts as soon as possible and replace with visual prompts
- Minimise or remove sensory triggers and adapt the physical environment by keeping colours and lighting muted, keeping noise to a minimum, avoiding smells that might trigger upset, reducing clutter, organising and labelling work spaces, signposting/symbolising, etc.
- Become familiar with, and look out for, signs of agitation e.g. tensing, pacing, hand-flapping, hand-biting, etc.
- Act upon these signs quickly to de-escalate stress, e.g. by allowing short periods of 'time out' away from the stressful environment. This might take the form of a short walk or five minutes with a favourite book. Such periods should be strictly time limited (perhaps using a visual egg timer for those who cannot read a clock) so that they do not reward avoidance

L for Links

Consistency is vital for individuals with autism, due to their heightened dislike of change and difficulty transferring knowledge and understanding from one context to another. Consistency is best facilitated by establishing strong links between all professionals involved with a client, the client themselves and their family and peers. Partnership working is clearly critical to this endeavour and should therefore underpin practice in all service contexts (Wall 2007). Indeed, this is recognised and enforced in autism legislation and policy across education, health, social care and the voluntary sector. This issue is discussed in more detail in chapter 5.

Making links:

- Maintain close links with parents/peers/professionals to share expertise, establish consistency and celebrate achievements
- Seek opportunities for inclusion in mainstream activities, community events, daily life activities, e.g. shopping
- Avoid exclusion by adapting the environment to enable participation

Summary

This section began with identification of some of the more commonly used interventions to support clients with autism. This was accompanied by a critical discussion of their evidence base, and the problem of the low status currently attributed to qualitative studies compared to quantitative studies. The strengths and limitations of both were explored and a case was made for a more integrated and balanced evidence base that draws from both research paradigms.

The popular SPELL framework was then explored in detail and reference was again made to the evidence underpinning claims for its efficacy. The importance of a structured approach to all aspects of support is highlighted by SPELL and was explored in relation to the physical, sensory, learning, communication and social context of the service environment. The value of positivity, empathy, low-arousal contexts and links across partners were also examined and justified.

Here are some of the key components of an effective intervention package:

- Individualising, assessing and adapting inputs
- Adapting the environment
- Structuring time, space and events
- Establishing consistency, predictability and routine
- Fading verbal/physical/gestural prompts
- Increasing visual supports and prompts
- Teaching specific cognitive, social and communication skills

- Being empathetic and person-centred
- Being collaborative

These are all considerations for practitioners when making decisions about client needs and how best to meet them. Indeed, SPELL is a useful acronym precisely because it prompts recall of these key features of good practice, ensuring that they are taken into account. To illustrate this, we will now consider how practitioners in a residential care context used SPELL to meet the needs of a client with autism.

SPELL in practice: case study in a social care context

Supporting Marshall

Jim is the manager of a social care service for clients with learning disabilities and complex needs. His role is to develop individualised services to enable clients to live as independently as possible in their own flats. Jim is also a SPELL trainer and supports staff to help clients develop the necessary life skills to lead a full and active life.

One of Jim's clients, Marshall, is 23 years old with a recent diagnosis of autism. For a long time, Marshall had struggled to understand his own needs and make sense of his experiences. When autism was finally diagnosed and explained using a social story, he initially rejected the idea. However, he slowly came to realise that he has no choice about his condition and began to understand that, with appropriate support, he could live the life he wanted.

Marshall enjoys music and has an excellent memory for all the bands he loves. He is very sociable, even though he struggles with social interaction, and he loves to host parties. He will always be the first one to get up and do karaoke to get everyone going! Marshall is kind-hearted and generous and he likes animals, particularly dogs. Marshall is hypersensitive to smells and some noises. He has difficulties with flexibility of thought and prefers to have no more than two choices. He learns well by rote and by copying others – even if the models around him are negative. He has a poor sleeping pattern and can demonstrate challenging behaviour when his anxieties are high. This behaviour can be directed at himself or others.

Marshall has been living in the service accommodation for approximately three years, and has his own flat with visiting support 24 hours a day, seven days a week. Initially, the visiting support was delivered by a large team who also supported a number of other individuals living within the same block. This meant that clients were sometimes competing for support at the same time. Staff turnover was high. Marshall struggled with this situation and often became highly anxious during support periods, resulting in challenging behaviour that soon escalated out of control. The outcome was invariably restrictive measures within his flat. Worryingly, it also sometimes resulted in intervention by the police and admittance to a secure unit.

When Jim joined the care service 12 months ago, he was alarmed to see Marshall trapped in such a deeply negative and destructive cycle. In response, he initiated a collaborative, person-centred assessment of Marshall's needs to be undertaken by a small, dedicated team who had received SPELL training. This team was fully informed of his needs and their task was to get to know Marshall better, building a more trusting relationship with him and enhance his support using SPELL principles based on the results of their assessment. Joint observations pinpointed the chaos and poor timing of previous staff support, plus poor visual structure and communication, as key issues.

The team began by introducing schedules to structure, organise and present Marshall's daily routines in a visual format he could understand. The day was broken down into short sections that he could manage, as the team realised that too much information was confusing for him. His poor concept of time further exacerbated this. A structured, low-arousal environment was therefore a high priority. The team also looked closely at Marshall's strengths and capitalised on these as a way of de-escalating anxiety. For example, they found that playing his favourite music and/or dancing with him had significant calming influence on Marshall, and was very effective in reducing stress. A daily recording system that monitored what worked for Marshall was introduced so that staff could note the strategies that helped him through stressful periods. This learning was then built into his daily routine.

The team is currently working with Marshall to find opportunities for increasing his participation in social activities, in order to give his life more meaning and purpose. For example, Marshall would like to create pub quizzes so that he can host his own one in a local venue. He would also like to help others by walking their dogs. Marshall is now more able to communicate what he wants to do with his life and, although he is still challenged by his sensory impairments, he is better able to deal with them as he is much more in control of his environment and generally more relaxed.

The focus on structure, positivity, empathetic support, low arousal and links to the local community are clearly emphasised in the support plan outlined above. Indeed, since implementing this plan 12 months ago, there has been no further police involvement and no referrals to the secure unit; Marshall is being supported fully using the SPELL framework. Interestingly, staff turnover has reduced and staff feedback suggests that supporting Marshall is now much more enjoyable. Working with the SPELL principles has clearly helped them all.

Jim commented: 'I'm an enthusiastic advocate of the SPELL framework as I have seen, over the last six years working with around 40 individuals, the benefits both to the individual and to the staff of being able to have more positive experiences and opportunities. As an aside I also feel that there is a really positive impact on the public purse as well. Marshall is now reaping the benefits by being able to participate more happily and meaningfully within his community with less paid support being required.'

Summary

This case provides insights into good autism practice and illustrates the value of timely, person-centred intervention based on the SPELL framework. The focus on visual structure as a means of facilitating communications, supporting understanding, lowering frustration and enabling participation and control, was clearly vital for Marshall, and helped to resolve a very challenging situation that threatened his well-being. The staff worked proactively and positively with Marshall without resorting to punitive methods. Indeed, they approached Marshall's predicament supportively, empathetically and flexibly, adjusting their practice in response to his needs and in light of the autism lens. They made links and sought consistency across the team via ongoing collaborative working.

It is notable, in this study, that deterioration in client behaviour and well-being was a decisive trigger for practitioner action. Note also that Jim did not blame Marshall for this or expect him to self-monitor or adapt to staff needs or context requirements. Rather his behaviour was read as a form of communication that triggered adjustments and adaptations to the environment around the client. The intervention had the direct effect of reducing Marshall's stress and the self-destructive behaviour that followed.

In the next chapter, we will explore this issue in much greater depth, looking more closely at a particular form of analysis, called functional analysis, that can be valuable in addressing so-called 'challenging behaviour'.

References

Aarons, M. & Gittens, T. (1992) *The Autistic Continuum*, London: NFER-Nelson.

Ashman, D. & Beadle-Brown, J. (2006) *A Valued Life*, London: United Response.

Ashton Smith, J. (2011) Mutual attraction? How do we identify and attract the right people to work in the field of autism? *Good Autism Practice*, 12/2, 43–50.

Barton, E.E., Lawrence, K. & Deurloo, F. (2011) Individualising interventions for young children with autism in preschool, *Journal of Autism and Developmental Disorders*, Online First, 18 Feb.

Beadle-Brown, J., Hutchinson, A. & Whelton, B. (2012) Person-Centred Active Support: increasing choice, promoting independence and reducing challenging behaviour, *Journal of Applied Research in Intellectual Disabilities*, 25, 291–307.

Biel, L. & Peske, N. (2005) *Raising a Sensory Smart Child*, New York: Penguin.

Bishop, D. (2003) *Children's Communication Checklist* (CCC-2), London: Pearson.

Black, P. & Wiliam, D. (1998) *Inside the Black Box: Raising Standards through Classroom Assessment*, London: King's College London School Of Education. Available: http://weaeducation.typepad.co.uk/files/blackbox-1.pdf (accessed March 2011).

Crabtree, J., Strydom, A. & Kirkpatrick, D. (2011) Community mental health professionals' knowledge and understanding of AS and the needs of this client group, *Good Autism Practice*, 12/2, 56–61.

Dakin, S. & Frith, U. (2005) Vagaries of visual perception, *Neuron*, 48, 497–507.

Daly, J. (2008) *I Exist: The message from Adults with Autism in Scotland*, Glasgow: National Autistic Society Scotland.

DCSF (Department for Children, Schools & Families) (2010) *Breaking the Link between Special Educational Needs &Low Attainment: Everyone's Business*. Available: http://publications.dcsf.gov.uk (accessed Feb 2012).

DoH (Department of Health) (2010) *Implementing Fulfilling and Rewarding Lives: Statutory Guidance for Local Authorities and NHS Organisations to Support Implementation of the Autism Strategy*, London: DoH.

Dunlop, A.W., Tait, C., Leask, A., Glashan, L., Robinson, A. & Marwick, H. (2009) *The Autism Toolbox: An Autism Resource for Scottish Schools*, Edinburgh: Scottish Government.

EADSNE (European Agency for Development in Special Needs Education (2009) *Assessment for Learning and Pupils with Special Educational Needs*. Available: http://www.european-agency.org/publications (accessed Feb 2012).

Francis, K. (2005) Autism interventions: a critical update, *Developmental Medicine & Child Neurology*, 47, 493–499.

Gilliam, J.E. (2001) *Gilliam Autism Rating Scale Second Edition* (GARS-2), Austin (USA): Pro-Ed.

Gilliam, J.E. (2005) *Gilliam Asperger's Diagnostic Scale* (GADS), Austin (USA): Pro-Ed.

Goldstein, S. & Naglieri, J.A. (2010) *Autism Spectrum Rating Scales* (ASRS), Los Angeles (USA): Western Psychological Services.

Goleman, D. (2007) *Three Kinds of Empathy: Cognitive, Emotional, Compassionate*. Available: http://danielgoleman.info/2007/three-kinds-of-empathy-cognitive-emotional-compassionate/ (accessed July 2012).

Grandin, T. (1995) *Thinking in Pictures: And Other Reports from My life With Autism*, London: Doubleday.

Happe, F. (2003) Theory of Mind and the Self, *Annals New York Academy of Sciences 1001*, 134–144.

HMIE (Her Majesty's Inspectorate of Education) (2006) *Education for Children with Autism Spectrum Disorders*, Edinburgh: HMIE.

Humphrey, N. & Lewis, S. (2008) What does 'inclusion' mean for pupils on the autistic spectrum in mainstream secondary schools? *Journal of Research in Special Educational Needs*, 8/3, 132–140.

Humphrey, N. & Parkinson, G. (2006) Research on interventions for children and young people on the autistic spectrum: a critical perspective, *Journal of Research in Special Educational Needs*, 6/2. 76–86.

Jones, G., English, A., Guldberg, K., Jordan, R., Richardson, P. & Waltz, M. (2009) *Educational Provision for Children and Young People on the Autism Spectrum Living in England: A Review of Current Practice, Issues and Challenges*, London: Autism Education Trust.

Leekham, S. & McGregor, E. (2008) Conclusion: integrating neurocognitive, diagnostic & intervention perspectives in autism, in E. McGregor, M. Núñez, K. Cebula & J.C. Gomez (eds), *Autism: An Integrated View From Neurocognitive, Clinical and Intervention Research*, London: Blackwell, 325–335.

Lord, C., Rutter, M.L. & LeCouteur, A. (1994) The Autism Diagnostic Interview – Revised (ADI-R), *Journal of Autism & Developmental Disorders*, 24, 659–685.

Lord, C., Rutter, M.L., Goode, S. & Heemshergen, J. (1989) Autism Diagnostic Observation Schedule: A standardised observation of communicative and social behaviour, *Journal of Autism & Developmental Disorders*, 19, 185–212.

Marco, E.J., Hinkley, L.B., Hill, S.S. & Nagarajan, S.S. (2011) Sensory processing in autism: a review of neurophysiologic findings, *Pediatric Research*, 69/5, 48–54.

Matson, J.L., Wilkins, J. & Gonzalez, M. (2007) Reliability and factor structure of ASD – diagnosis scale for intellectually disabled adults (ASD-DA), *Journal of Developmental and Physical Disabilities*, 19, 565–577.

McGregor, E., Núñez, M., Cebula, K. & Gomez, J.C. (2008) Introduction: seeking coherence in autism: from fMRI to intervention, in E. McGregor, M. Núñez, K. Cebula & J.C. Gomez (eds), *Autism: An Integrated View From Neurocognitive, Clinical and Intervention Research*, London: Blackwell, 1–19.

Mesibov, G.B. & Shea, V. (2010) The TEACCH Program in the era of evidence-based practice, *Journal of Autism & Developmental Disorders*, 40/5, 570–579.

Mesibov, G., Schopler, E., Schaffer, B. & Landrus, R. (1989) *Adolescent and Adult Psychoeducational Profile* (APEP), Austin (USA): Pro-Ed.

Mills, R. (2013) *Guidance for Considering a Treatment Approach to Autism.* Accessible: http://www.autism.org.uk/living-with-autism/strategies-and-approaches/before-choosing-an-approach/guidance-for-considering-a-treatment-approach-in-autism.aspx (accessed Oct. 2014).

Mills, R. & Marchant, S. (2011) Intervention in autism: a brief review of the literature, *Tizard Learning Disability Review*, 16/4, 20–35.

National Autistic Society (NAS) (updated April 2014) SPELL website. Accessible: http://www.autism.org.uk/Living-with-autism/Strategies-and-approaches/SPELL.aspx (accessed July 2014).

NICE (National Institute for Health & Clinical Excellence) (2011) *Autism: Recognition, Referral & the Diagnosis of Children and Young People on the Autism Spectrum*, London: NICE.

Ozonoff, S. & Cathcart, K. (1998) Effectiveness of a home programme intervention for young children with autism, *Journal of Autism and Developmental Disorders*, 28/1, 25–32.

Peeters, T. & Jordan, R. (1999) What makes a 'good' practitioner in the field of autism? *Good Autism Practice*, Birmingham: University of Birmingham.

PHIS (Public Health Institute of Scotland) (2001) *Autistic Spectrum Disorders: Needs Assessment Report*, Glasgow: PHIS.

Ravet, J. (2011) Inclusion/exclusion? Contradictory perspectives on autism and inclusion: the case for an integrative approach, *International Journal of Inclusive Education*, 15/6, 667–682.

Ravet, J. (2013) Delving deeper into the black box: formative assessment, inclusion and learners on the autism spectrum, *International Journal of Inclusive Education*, 17/9, 948–964.

Rosenblatt, M. (2008) *I Exist: The Message from Adults with Autism in England*, London: National Autistic Society.

Schopler, E., Mesibov, G.B. & Hearsy, K. (1995) Structured teaching in the TEACCH system, in E. Schopler & G.M. Mesibov (eds), *Learning & Cognition in Autism*, New York: Plenum Press.

Schopler, E., Lansing, M., Reichler, R. & Marcus, L. (2004) *Psychoeducational Profile Third Edition* (PEP-3), Austin (USA): Pro-Ed.

Schopler, E., Reichler, R.T., DeVellis, R. & Daly, K. (1980) Towards objective classification of childhood autism: Childhood Autism Rating Scale (CARS), *Journal of Autism & Developmental Disorders*, 10, 91–103.

Scottish Executive (2006) *Autistic Spectrum Disorders Needs Assessment Report (2001); Scottish Executive Report in Implementation and Next Steps*, Edinburgh: Scottish Executive.

Scottish Government (2011) *The Scottish Strategy for Autism*. Available: www.scotland.gov.uk (accessed April 2012).

Siasperas, P. & Beadle-Brown, J. (2006) The effectiveness of the TEACCH approach programme for people with autism in Greece, *Autism*, 10/4, 330–343.

SIGN (Scottish Intercollegiate Guidelines Network) (2007/2012) *Assessment, Diagnosis and Clinical Interventions for Children and Young People with Autism Spectrum Disorders: A National Clinical Guideline*, Edinburgh: SIGN.

Silver, K. (2005) *Assessing and Developing Communication and Thinking Skills in People with Autism and Communication Difficulties: A toolkit for parents and professionals*, London: Jessica Kingsley.

Stancliffe, R. J., Harman, A., Toogood, S. & McVilly, K.R. (2007) Australian implementation and evaluation of active support, *Journal of Applied Research in Intellectual Disabilities*, 20, 211–227.

Wall, K. (2007) *Education and Care for Adolescents and Adults with Autism: A Guide for Professionals and Carers*, London: Sage.

Wilkinson, K. & Twist, L. (2010) *Autism & Educational Assessment: UK Policy and Practice*, Berkshire: NFER.

Wing, L., Leekham, S.R., Libby, S.J., Gould, J. & Larcombe, M. (2002) The diagnostic interview for social and communication disorders: background, inter-rater reliability and clinical use, *Journal of Child Psychology & Psychiatry*, 43, 307–325.

Woodbury-Smith, M. R. & Volkmar, F.R. (2009) Asperger's Syndrome: a review, *European Child & Adolescent Psychiatry*, 18, 2–11.

Chapter 4

Making sense of behaviour

There is a widespread belief, supported by research evidence, that a diagnosis of autism, especially when accompanied by severe intellectual disability, is associated with enhanced risk of 'challenging behaviour' (McClintock et al. 2003, McTiernan et al. 2011). This potent correlation raises a number of important questions:

- What does the term 'challenging behaviour' actually mean?
- Why does this negative association exist?
- What are the implications of challenging behaviour?
- How can it be addressed?

In this chapter, each of these questions will be critically examined in order to explore why behaviour can be problematic for individuals with autism, caregivers and professionals, and why, as we shall see, it is a major cause of exclusion across many service settings. A case study from an education setting will be included to illustrate some of the complexities involved and to showcase how practitioners can address and reduce challenging behavioural in the workplace.

What is 'challenging' behaviour?

There are several problems with the notion of 'challenging' behaviour:

a) Confusingly, in the literature, this term tends to be used synonymously with a range of other terms such as maladapted behaviour, difficult behaviour, problem behaviour, disruptive behaviour or unwanted behaviour. These terms are rarely distinguished or consistently defined.
b) Across the literature, challenging behaviour is variously associated with anti-social behaviour (e.g. smearing faeces, masturbating in public), aggression towards others (e.g. hitting, spitting), self-harm (e.g. biting oneself, head-banging), stereotypies (e.g. hand-flapping, body-rocking), tantrums (e.g. fits of shouting or screaming), defiance (e.g. refusal to eat,

avoiding demands), disruption (e.g. interfering with others, failing to observe social rules) or destruction (e.g. throwing things, causing damage to property). However, there is little consistency as to which features apply and, often, little information about their intensity, frequency or duration. This makes comparison and generalisation difficult.

c) People's tolerances for different behaviours vary considerably, which means that their behaviour ratings are highly subjective. Thus, a behaviour that is considered 'challenging' by one person may be merely irritating to another, which may have an impact on the behaviour itself. Cultural differences may also be significant (Chung et al. 2012). This leads to further inconsistency in the use of the term.

d) Arguably, the term 'challenging behaviour' contains within it the a priori assumption that the behaviour is somehow deliberately, intentionally or inherently challenging. It therefore implies that the 'problem' is located firmly in the person presenting the behaviour, rather than in the environment in which it takes place. As we shall see, this assumption is far from reliable.

Challenging behaviour is therefore a thorny subject. The lack of consensus around terminology and meaning, and other inconsistencies in the application of the term, suggests that we must be careful in our use of it, and cautious in our reading of the literature and research in the field. I would prefer not to use the term challenging behaviour at all. However, finding an alternative term raises similar issues. The terms difficult behaviour, unwanted behaviour, disruptive behaviour, etc. are all equally problematic. An alternative would be to simply talk about 'behaviour'. However, this chapter is not about behaviour in general but about the forms of behaviour that tend to cause service breakdowns and lead quickly to exclusion. 'Challenging' is the term widely used in the literature, and even more widely used in practice settings, for the sort of behaviour we will be discussing.

Thus, for the purposes of this book, the term challenging behaviour will be retained and taken to mean behaviours that are socially unacceptable, dangerous to self and others and which impact negatively on everyday experiences, quality of life and life chances (Emerson 2001, Jang et al. 2011). However, the word 'challenging', it should be emphasised, refers to the behaviours in question, *not* to individuals.

Why is autism associated with challenging behaviour?

The strong link between autism and challenging behaviour is attributed to a range of factors in the research. It is well established that severe and profound intellectual disability is a major risk marker for challenging behaviour (Holden & Gitlesen 2006), but when combined with autism and related communication difficulties, the association is strengthened and correlated, in particular, to self-injury, stereotypies, aggression and destruction of property (McClintock et al. 2003, McTiernan et al. 2011). A diagnosis of autism towards the severe and complex end of the spectrum is therefore predictive of challenging behaviour. By contrast, diagnoses of high-functioning autism and Asperger's Syndrome are associated with 'lower frequency and severity of challenging behaviour' (McTiernan et al. 2011, p. 1221).

Other studies make specific links between increased risk of challenging behaviour and the severity of ASD (without intellectual disability) (Jang et al. 2011), perseverative behaviour and sensory disturbance (Reece et al. 2003), problems with expressive communication (Chiang 2008), and temperament (Adamek et al. 2011). Contrary to popular belief, gender has not been established as a risk marker for challenging behaviour within the autism community (Holden & Gitlesen 2006, McTiernan et al. 2011). Findings for other risk factors, such as age and impact of early intervention, have so far proved ambiguous (ibid.).

Challenging behaviour of one form or another is thought to be exhibited by 'about half' of individuals with a diagnosis of autism spectrum conditions (Chung et al. 2012). There is significant evidence that children and adolescents with autism are more likely to display challenging behaviour compared to typically developing individuals and those with psychopathology, learning disability or learning impairments (Matson et al. 2010). There is also evidence that challenging behaviour has a tendency to persist and become 'chronic' (ibid.).

These research findings therefore confirm a strong correlation between autism and challenging behaviour. However, this should not be surprising given the core deficits of the condition and the struggles they imply. The constellation of social and communication difficulties associated with autism, coupled with rigidity of thought, repetitive behaviour, sensory issues, and exacerbated by learning difficulties, inevitably brings significant potential for fear, anger, stress, frustration and upset during everyday interaction in everyday contexts. The sheer complexity of the condition, compounded by individual variability, heightens this potential.

Consider, for a moment, the impact of the three core features of autism:

- If a person lacks communication skills, they will find it extremely difficult to express their pain, physical discomfort, sensory sensations, thoughts and opinions, emotions, wants, needs and desires. They may also have difficulty with receptive communication and fail to understand incoming information, interactions, questions, instructions, etc.
- If they lack social understanding they will find it difficult to play, form relationships, interact and participate in everyday social contexts and at social events.

- If they lack flexibility they will find it difficult to cope with change, transitions, unpredictable events, choices and decisions.

Individuals with autism regularly experience potent combinations of several of these potential stressors. Imagine how complex, confusing and overwhelming this must be. To add to this, these internal triggers may be obscure to others, and difficult to isolate, identify and address. It is little wonder that people with autism are especially vulnerable to behavioural outbursts.

But this is not the full picture...

Undeniably, some behavioural triggers are internal. However, it is vital to appreciate that challenging behaviour does not happen in a vacuum. It almost always arises at particular moments, in specific contexts, usually amongst others and in response to a variety of external triggers. In fact, most challenging behaviour is 'over-determined', i.e. it arises from a combination of internal and external triggers. If we can identify at least some of these triggers, then we have a chance of minimising their impact on individuals with autism and reducing the incidence of challenging behaviour. It is not, therefore, appropriate to blame people with autism for challenging behaviour. Rather, the behaviour should be considered socially constructed in the sense that the antecedents of the behaviour are frequently found in the social context in which it occurs and its development directly influenced by the subjective interpretations and responses of others. We discuss this in more detail below.

Challenging behaviour is not, therefore, an inevitability. However, it is a very real and highly significant issue for many individuals with autism and for the carers and the professionals who support them, not least because of its profound implications for social and intellectual development, health and well-being.

The implications of challenging behaviour

Challenging behaviour that occurs at high levels of intensity, frequency and duration is likely to be debilitating for individuals with autism and for those supporting them who witness it, may become embroiled in it, and must cope with it whilst keeping clients, themselves and others safe. Incidents of serious challenging behaviour are, without doubt, discomfiting and upsetting for all involved, and can put considerable strain on service provision.

Implications for individuals with autism include:

- Physical injury, infection, physical malformation, loss of sight/hearing, neurological damage

- Social and academic exclusion, social isolation, rejection by peers and family, delayed adaptive, social and intellectual development, home/school/care-service/employment breakdown
- Increased use of physical restraint, psychotropic drugs, intrusive treatments, police involvement, institutionalisation, hospitalisation

Implications for caregivers, families, professionals and service providers include:

- Physical injury, physical and mental stress and exhaustion, loss of coping, isolation, damage to property, family breakdown, staff burnout, staff losses, increased costs
                    (McDonnell et al. 2008, McTiernan et al. 2011,
                         Chung et al. 2012, Weiss et al. 2012)

The impact of challenging behaviour should not, therefore, be underestimated. This highlights the importance of positive behaviour support across care contexts and wider service provision, to which we now turn.

Addressing challenging behaviour

The way that families and professionals approach challenging behaviour depends very much on their theoretical perspective and also on underlying values and beliefs. For example, if the behaviour is viewed as an attitude problem, then a punishment may be sought; if it is perceived as a medical problem, then drug treatment may be sought; if it is considered a psychological problem, then therapy may be sought; if it is judged to be a learning issue, then an educational programme may be sought (Whitaker 2001). All of these approaches have value and validity in specific circumstances. However, some may provide only short-term solutions as they do not yield insights into the underlying meaning of the behaviour. Others require specialist knowledge in specialist settings and cannot be undertaken across service contexts or in the home. Punitive interventions may be at risk of compromising the dignity and rights of individuals with autism unless professionalism is carefully monitored. In any situation where the views of individuals with autism are not taken fully into account, there is a risk that power issues enter the equation and, in the worst cases, that people on the autism spectrum are subject to gross or subtle coercion and practices devoid of human understanding and compassion. Sadly, we need only open the newspapers to be reminded that such practices are far from rare.

In this chapter we will therefore confine our discussion to 'positive behaviour support' – an approach that, in theory at least, is inclusive, person-centred, collaborative, preventative, and provides practical solutions that can be incorporated into everyday routines in the home, care setting, community and other everyday contexts (Marshall & Mirenda 2002) .

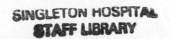

Positive behaviour support: what is it?

> The signature feature of positive behaviour support (is) a committed focus on fixing environments, not people
>
> (Horner 2000, p. 97).

The notion of positive behaviour support is not unique to the field of autism but has emerged from a long tradition of research and practice into the factors that influence human behaviour and how behaviour change occurs (Horner 2000). It might be defined as 'the application of behaviour analysis to the social problems created by (challenging) behaviour' (ibid., p. 97). Positive behaviour support proceeds in a manner that respects the rights and dignity of people with disabilities by avoiding use of approaches that are punitive and coercive. In their seminal paper, Horner et al. (1990) argued that aversive approaches result in humiliation, isolation and shame whilst having little impact on the behaviour itself.

Instead, positive behaviour support starts from the premise that *all behaviour is a form of communication* and therefore has a purpose or function. It seeks to identify this function using 'functional assessment':

> a respectful process of trying to understand when, where, and why (an individual) engages in problem behaviour. It is respectful in that the process adopts the perspective of the person with the problem behaviours. The assumption is not that individuals are defective or broken, but that they experience the world around them in a way that is different from their peers...the challenge of assessment (is) one of first understanding that perspective.
>
> (Horner 2000, p. 99)

The aim of functional assessment is to identify a person's strengths and preferences, understand their communication strategy, and establish the antecedents and consequences of the challenging behaviour in the environment in which it takes place. This information is used to adapt the environment in order to alter the usual course of the behaviour, and thereby reduce, modify or eliminate the need for it. The ultimate aim is to create contexts in which the individual, and everyone else, can be 'productive and safe' (Horner 2000, p. 103).

Let us take the example of Mary.

Mary is an extremely bright, articulate and engaging 12-year-old girl with Asperger's Syndrome who has a history of frequent and intense outbursts of stereotypical behaviour involving repetitive body movements accompanied by shouting, crying and unusual noises. Mary's behaviour is not harmful to herself or anyone else, but when it starts it is difficult to stop, it is upsetting and frustrating for Mary, her carers and teachers, and it is disruptive of her social life, learning at school and the learning of others around her.

For years, Mary's family and the professionals supporting her tried to stop Mary's stereotypies by using traditional behaviour management strategies such as telling her off, trying to ignore the behaviour, and providing rewards for good behaviour. However, none of these interventions made the slightest difference, or made matters worse.

Positive behaviour support was then introduced and a functional assessment was undertaken to analyse where, when and why Mary's stereotypies tended to manifest. It was soon discovered that they were generally triggered when a new activity was introduced, especially one that took place in a new room or context she wasn't used to, and which involved new people, e.g. going to the swimming pool or restaurant, starting a new topic at school, or moving to a new class with a new teacher. The assessment revealed that the behaviour seemed to be a way of communicating fear and ensuring withdrawal from, and therefore avoidance of, the threat of the new experience. It was Mary's way of taking control without words.

Since traditional behaviour management approaches had not worked, without being aware of it everyone around Mary reinforced her challenging behaviour by removing her very quickly from the contexts that upset her in order to bring the behaviour to an end. As a result, the behaviour was repeated frequently whenever a new experience approached. This ensured that Mary avoided new experiences and calmed down. However, it also meant that she was increasingly isolated from peers and made little social and academic progress. Everyone began to feel trapped and frustrated.

Mary's behaviour began to subside as soon as the autism lens was applied and the environment was adapted to meet Mary's needs. A daily schedule was designed to give Mary advance warning that a new activity was soon to be started, time was taken to explain what would happen, photographs of the new context were prepared, and plans were made to visit the context in advance and phase the context and new activities in slowly so that Mary had time to acclimatise to them. These steps were taken, systematically, every time a new experience was introduced.

These simple changes meant that there was less need for the stereotypies and they therefore reduced in frequency and intensity. Mary was not 'fixed' in this process, but, by seeing the world through her eyes and applying the autism lens, the resources, organisation and the responses of the people around her were transformed. The environment was significantly modified. This made all the difference in the world to Mary.

This scenario illustrates the key features of positive behaviour support, at the heart of which lies functional assessment. The focus on modifying the environment, rather than Mary, is absolutely central to this approach. Let us look at this more closely to see what it entails and explore its evidence base.

Functional assessment

According to Marshall & Mirenda (2002), functional assessment has several phases:

> **Phase 1**: Establishing collaborative partnerships
> **Phase 2**: Conducting the functional assessment
> o   Identifying behaviours of concern
> o   Conducting the functional assessment
> o   Developing collaborative hypotheses
> **Phase 3**: Developing a collaborative behaviour support plan
> **Phase 4**: Implementing and monitoring the behaviour support plan

Phase 1. Establishing collaborative relationships

For functional assessment to be effective it needs to be collaborative, so it must begin by building strong relationships amongst all parties involved in supporting the individual showing challenging behaviour and must, wherever possible, include the individual themselves. Establishing trust, positive regard and mutual understanding are pre-requisites for the effective functioning of the collaborative group, and time needs to be invested in establishing these qualities.

Everyone must be involved in gathering data for the assessment so that there is joint understanding, joint ownership of the behaviour support plan that results, consistency of application, and joint responsibility for outcomes. This approach also facilitates joint learning and the development of a viable community of support throughout the duration of the assessment and beyond.

Phase 2. Conducting the functional assessment

a) Identifying behaviours of concern

Reference has already been made to the fact that perceptions of behaviour are highly subjective. It is therefore important that decisions about the focus of positive behaviour support are agreed amongst all those involved in the care of the client concerned through a process of joint information sharing, negotiation and decision-making. This ensures a consensus about behaviour priorities and minimises that possibility of one individual using their power to control the client, or the group, in order to meet their own needs or agenda.

b) Conducting the functional assessment

Above, it was stated that the aim of functional assessment is to identify a person's strengths and preferences, understand their communication strategy, and establish the antecedents and consequences of the challenging behaviour in the environment in which it takes place. This can be achieved by using a functional assessment interview and conducting a functional assessment observation.

THE FUNCTIONAL ASSESSMENT INTERVIEW

The aim of the functional assessment interview is to gather the following information:

- Descriptions of the behaviour
- Details of the setting in which the behaviour generally takes place
- Details of antecedents, i.e. events, situations or people in the setting that trigger or precede the behaviour
- Details of consequences that might indicate the function of the behaviour

The interview is conducted with the client with autism and everyone around the client involved in their care – especially those who are regularly present when the challenging behaviour takes place. The information gathered from the interview is then used to generate hypotheses about the meaning of the challenging behaviour and its communicative function from the point of view of the client. Those analysing the information and generating hypotheses must therefore have a sound grasp of autism, must be able to use the autism lens, and must be able to empathetically step into the client's shoes.

THE FUNCTIONAL ASSESSMENT OBSERVATION

The aim of the functional assessment observation is to gather further information that might help to validate or invalidate the hypotheses generated by the functional assessment interviews, and to provide additional insights that might facilitate refinement of the developing hypothesis. The observations should take place when the challenging behaviour occurs and be written up immediately after, whenever possible. An observation schedule should be used to enable the observer to collect a range of useful data:

- Setting
- Time of day
- Who was present
- What happened
- Antecedents
- The behaviour and its apparent function
- Consequences

These observations are best undertaken a number of times, by different people, in the various setting in which the behaviour usually takes place, so that as much direct observational data are generated as possible. A tool commonly used to collect this data is the STAR chart (box 4.1) (see Zarkowska & Clements 1994). It is vital that the observation data is recorded as objectively as possible and without interpretation or judgment, e.g. 'the client then kicked the carer', not 'the client was then very aggressive'.

Box 4.1: The STAR model

S Setting: details of time, context, environment and people present when the incident takes place

T Trigger: the event or sequence of actions that precede the behaviour

A Action: what the person actually does

R Results: the outcome or aftermath of the behaviour

STAR Format and Exemplar:

SETTING	TRIGGER	ACTION	RESULT
• Changing rooms at swimming pool (10.30 a.m.) • Six young people in group, each getting changed in separate cubicles • Two helpers going between cubicles • A few members of the public (adults and children) • Strong smell of chlorine • Very hot and sweaty • Noisy (children laughing and running in and out of showers) • Floors very wet • Cubicles small and quite dark • First visit for several months	Young people are asked to get undressed and put on their swimming costumes. Anna is reminded several times but sits on the bench with eyes closed and hands over ears. Helper tries to assist.	Anna tries to bite helper's hand, hits and pushes past helper and runs out of door through foyer into car park. Anna returns to waiting bus and tries to get in.	Taken to observation area, given drink and crisps. Helper sits with Anna for the rest of the swimming session. Anna calms down quickly, smiles, laughs, and seems happy to watch and wave to her friends.

c) Developing collaborative hypotheses

When the interview and observation data have been gathered, it must be systematically analysed to reveal repetitive patterns that suggest explanations for the behaviour:

- **Notice the setting**: e.g. does the behaviour occur at around the same time, in the same location or with the same people, during a particular activity, during any sort of transition or a particular sort of transition?
- **Notice the antecedents**: e.g. is the behaviour triggered by fear, anger, feeling overwhelmed, confusion, a want or desire, an external demand, an unscheduled change, a sensory stimulus?
- **Notice the consequences**: e.g. does the behaviour always result in attention, removal of a demand, gratification of a want or desire, sensory stimulation, some sort of reward?

These patterns then form the basis of a hypotheses or theory about the meaning of the behaviour. For example, is it a way of expressing thoughts or feelings; an escape or avoidance strategy; a way of satisfying a want or need?

It is important to note that the process of collaborative problem solving and joint analysis is not always straightforward, as different interpretations of the data may arise and have to be sensitively handled and carefully negotiated. There is not always an obvious 'right answer' to the problem. To complicate things further, there may also be multiple triggers involved.

O'Neill et al. (1997) suggest that summary statements that integrate the key details of the data can help to create a succinct hypothesis. The statements can take the following form:

> *When (antecedent) occurs, (person) is likely to (behaviour) in order to (consequence/function). This is more likely to occur if (setting event).*

When applied to Mary's case, the statement might read as follows:

> *When Mary is presented with a new activity that she has never tried before, she is likely to engage in stereotypical behaviour in order to avoid the demand. This is more likely to occur if she is fearful, has never done the activity before and if it takes place in a different room or context with lots of peers in the vicinity.*

One or several of these statements may be generated at this stage, and then further integrated.

Phase 3. Developing a collaborative behaviour support plan

In this phase, the aim is to draw on the hypotheses, and the wealth of data gathered from the interviews and observations, to construct a behaviour support plan. It should now go without saying that this must be approached collaboratively. To be effective, the plan must set out a clear strategy to address the components identified in the summary statements so that the challenging behaviour becomes *irrelevant, inefficient or ineffective* (Marshall & Mirenda 2002). In other words, the plan should render the behaviour unnecessary by creating new and more constructive ways of achieving the same pay-off or by introducing a new pay-off. Unfortunately, there is no formula for this; it might be achieved in any number of ways, e.g. by modifying aspects of the setting, structuring learning demands, introducing new skills, providing new motivators, creating new rules, etc. Often a combination of interventions is required. The next step is therefore to collaboratively generate a list of interventions to address the underlying problem.

In Mary's case the underlying problem was her fear of new experiences, especially those taking place in new contexts with new people around her. To circumvent this fear, and to avoid the need for the challenging behaviour, staff used various interventions such as a daily schedule, visual supports, visits and a phasing strategy. These were all used to ease Mary very slowly into new experiences and encounters in a way that would allay her fears and enable her to cope. These interventions were used systematically by all staff, in all contexts, at all times, so that they became habitual and predictable, and embedded in Mary's everyday routine. This empowered Mary, enabling her to feel in control and gain the confidence she needed to enter more calmly into new experiences where she could begin, at last, to learn and to socialise with others.

Box 4.2 provides an example of a behaviour support plan for Mary using a typical template.

Phase 4. Implementing and monitoring the behaviour support plan

Successful implementation of the behaviour support plan relies on effective dissemination and communication and must include, as a priority, collaborative discussion. It is vital that everyone agrees to the plan and is fully familiar with the intervention requirements. Since the devil is always in the detail, discussion of the nuances of the plan is important to ensure that each element is fully understood and enacted in consistent fashion. It is also important that interventions are matched to the context. This is referred to in the literature as 'social validity' (Wolf 1978). If an intervention has social validity, it is deemed, by those who must implement it, to be socially acceptable within the contexts in which it will be used, and will fit easily into its natural routines. Such interventions have a much better chance of success (Machalicek et al. 2006).

Box 4.2: Behaviour support plan for Mary

Triggers:	Proactive interventions:	Early warning signs:	Escalation behaviours:	Crisis interventions:
New experiences e.g. new learning activity, taking a new route to school, any change of routine **New people** e.g. new teachers, support assistants or peers **New contexts** e.g. first visit to a hairdresser, after-school club, doctor, etc.	**These strategies will help to minimise stress and avoid upset:** Highlight changes to routine on Mary's visual schedule Discuss changes or new experiences in advance using visual supports (photographs are best) and a social story Phase in the change very slowly, e.g. keep new learning activities/experiences very short and reward quickly on completion Reward using favourite book, using visual egg timer at first (three minutes only) Use visual supports to move on to next task Slowly **fade** reward so that Mary learns to move from new task/experience straight back into routine	**If a new experience or change of routine occurs without preparation, Mary will begin to feel distressed:** Rocking and gentle, low-level repetitive body movements Soft whimpering noises Head down – avoidance of eye contact **These are signs that there is a problem in the environment and more visual structure is required to avoid escalation** i.e. slow down pace, reduce interaction, use more visual support, create a social story, reduce demand and use a phasing strategy to introduce tasks slowly	**If early warning signs are ignored:** Body movements will increase and intensify, e.g. Head down, eyes closed Breathing speeds up considerably and audibly Loud shouting and crying with a great deal of distress She will not hear instructions and may place hands over ears She may run around in a frantic way or drop to floor	Stop any activity or interaction Speak to Mary in a very calm, reassuring tone (avoid aversive responses). Do not touch Mary Give 'quiet-time' card (avoid instructions) Place book and timer nearby. Point to quiet area/floor cushion and give her time to go herself. Avoid helping Allow time for de-escalation (Mary usually sleeps for a few minutes) When breathing returns to normal and Mary looks up and around, provide water Avoid too much interaction/contact Provide visual support to indicate next task and move on

However, the durability and sustainability of a behaviour support plan is often an issue (Clements & Zarkowska 2000). After the initial burst of enthusiasm, those supporting an individual with autism may become lax and complacent so that adherence to the details of the arrangements begins to weaken. This is especially likely where several people are involved over a number of contexts. There is also the problem that aspects of the interventions may stop working. This may be for a wide variety of reasons, e.g. because the client stops responding to certain elements, such as a particular visual symbol, or does not respond positively to a particular person in the team. Such developments can trigger a downward spiral back into challenging behaviour which lowers morale and further undermines effectiveness. At this point the behaviour support plan can easily be relegated to the dustbin, landing everyone back at square one.

In order to avoid these outcomes it is important that the plan is regularly monitored and revised where necessary. It should be viewed as a working document on the clear understanding that it will inevitably have to be refined over time as things change. Thus monitoring should be built in to planning from the start to ensure longevity.

In monitoring the behaviour support plan, what matters is that the interventions are doing the job they were intended to do: the provision of positive behaviour support to enable successful inclusion and participation and the fulfilment of potential. The plan should be given time to work – at least a month. If challenging behaviour is reduced, minimised or eliminated within this time frame, this clearly suggests that the plan is being effective and will be cause for relief and celebration! If, however, there is no change, or if, over time, behaviours that were reduced, minimised or eliminated start to re-appear, or new forms of challenging behaviour start to emerge, this suggests the need for further action. This might take the form of a firming up of procedures that may have become slack, training in support interventions for new personnel, slight tweaks to planned interventions so that they work more effectively, the introduction of a supplementary intervention or a full-scale re-assessment of the situation, depending on circumstances. If nothing is done, one can reliably assume that the situation will deteriorate and that everyone's hard work will begin to unravel. Effective monitoring is an insurance against this outcome, and is well worth the effort.

Evidence base

There is considerable support in the practice community for this approach to challenging behaviour, not least because it is person-centred, preventative, protects dignity and rights, promotes inclusion and participation and seeks to enhance physical, mental and emotional well-being, social and intellectual development and quality of life. It is difficult to argue with such a long list of laudable aims.

There also is a growing body of research evidence that the approach works (e.g. McLean & Grey 2012, Durand et al. 2013, Preece 2014). This may be attributed to the fact that the principles of the approach are surprisingly simple, it is relatively easy to operationalise and can yield positive results very quickly after implementation. By its very essence, this approach focuses on those environmental factors that can be changed, and avoids those factors that can't. This means that energy is used positively and that there is always potential for hope and success.

But success depends, of course, on the quality of the functional assessment, the effectiveness of collaborative working, the appropriateness of selected interventions, and the efficacy of implementation and ongoing monitoring. Positive behaviour support therefore calls for a willingness to reflect critically upon practice, without defensiveness, in order to identify the ongoing strengths and weaknesses in support provision.

In the case study to follow we will see how positive behaviour support is brought to life in a mainstream school.

Case study

Frances is a secondary teacher who supports pupils with additional support needs in a mainstream school with an autism base. Martin, a pupil with Asperger's Syndrome, came to the base from his primary school with a history of violent outbursts that he was unable to control. This was dealt with by two support assistants using formal restraint procedures. The crisis plan and risk assessment drawn up at the primary school transferred with Martin to his secondary placement. However, he settled down well during his first year in the secondary autism base. He had an individualised timetable, trusting relationships with staff and was included in small-group learning. The crisis plan was not required during this period. By the second year, Martin was feeling so happy, settled and secure in the base that he felt he might be able to attend some mainstream classes. Frances agreed that further inclusion would be appropriate.

In order to meet Martin's wish, Frances involved him and his parents in identifying his strengths and interests and tried to match these to mainstream classes that might accommodate his needs. Mainstream staff and support staff were consulted, adaptations to the mainstream teaching and learning environment were arranged, and Martin began to attend his new classes. In line with the risk assessment undertaken in primary school, Martin was accompanied to all classes by two personal support assistants (PSAs).

Despite some early anxiety, all was well until the third term of his placement in mainstream. At this point Martin became unsettled, agitated and anxious. He became increasingly aggressive when frustrated with his work, making loud noises and banging the table. Sometimes his aggression turned on other pupils and staff. This was highly unsettling for all the pupils and staff involved and regularly disrupted the learning environment. Though the PSAs attempted to intervene early to prevent escalation into aggression, their efforts proved ineffective and the outbursts continued. Frances recognised at this point that the support staff were trying to manage and control Martin's behaviour without fully understanding its cause. She realised that it was necessary to find out more about what might be triggering the outbursts.

She proceeded as follows:

1   She called an emergency meeting to discuss the issues with all those involved in Martin's care plan: his parents, teachers, outreach worker, voluntary worker and school managers. This was necessary to clarify roles and responsibilities and to negotiate a way forward.

2   Frances also spent a lot of time with Martin, supporting him to communicate his emotions, frustrations and possible triggers for his increasingly challenging behaviour. Issues were explored visually using diagrams and posters. In these sessions it became clear that Martin enjoyed his mainstream classes but felt 'different' and not part of the class. This was exacerbated by the two PSAs who 'over-supported' him, pointed out all his mistakes and drew attention to him. Martin also felt that these two members of staff did not like him. He stated that he would prefer not to have any staff working closely with him.

3   In order to investigate triggers further, an ABC functional analysis was used to gather data on antecedents and consequences, plus details about the environment at the time of each incident. Instruction was given to all staff in how to complete the ABC analysis. The results showed that aggressive outbursts were more likely when the two support staff were present. It also showed that he was allowed to leave class after each outburst and go back to the autism base to complete work at his personal work station. His outbursts therefore ensured that he could escape from the mainstream classroom, thus reinforcing the behaviour.

4   All of the above information was collated and discussed at a further collaborative meeting. Here Martin's mother confirmed that he had been stressed by the negative relationship between himself and the two support assistants. The following action was taken in order to address Martin's need more effectively, ensure safety and also address Martin's request for greater independence:

- The two support assistants were replaced and restorative work was planned to repair their relationship with Martin.
- The risk assessment was changed so that only one member of staff would provide support. This assistant would also provide general support for the class so that their focus was not solely on Martin.
- Instead of using physical restraint in the event of an aggressive outburst, other skills and coping strategies would be put in place. However, for safety, the support assistant would carry a walkie-talkie and follow crisis response protocols should an outburst be imminent.
- The senior management team (SMT) in the school would respond to incidents through the agreed channel.
- Roles and responsibilities were discussed and clarified with all staff supporting Martin.
- The plan was to be monitored for a month and then reviewed.

5   When the plan was reviewed it was clear that there had been immediate benefits. Martin enjoyed the reduced and more 'hands-off' support, the aggressive outbursts diminished and he was staying in class more. His relationship with the PSA was also more relaxed and interactive. However, the assistant noted that there were occasions when there was no response to the emergency calls to SMT. The assistant also found that her relationship with Martin could be intense and that more changes of staff would be helpful.

As a result of the review, rehearsals of the crisis response protocols were arranged, more PSAs became involved in Martin's support plan, and updates to Martin's care plan were circulated. Frances felt that the school behaviour and inclusion policies needed to be updated so that they addressed the needs of pupils with autism. She also recognised that further training was required, especially for mainstream teaching staff. This would enable them to use the autism lens to support all pupils with autism and help to create an ethos of acceptance and inclusion for all.

Summary

The case study above exemplifies what happens when challenging behaviour arises but the focus is on environmental change rather than 'fixing' the individual with autism. This fundamental shift is vital to the success of the positive behaviour support model. Frances acknowledges that functional assessment was pivotal to the success of her intervention as it enabled her to 'monitor the triggers for his behaviour and ... make suppositions about them.' These suppositions, or hypotheses, then enabled the team to explore alternative ways of addressing Martin's needs, thereby reducing his reliance on communication through aggression.

However, collaborative working is also at the heart of the model, as Frances points out: 'The reason that the changes implemented were so effective can be attributed to collaborative working and effective, honest communication. Martin was also included in this process and given a voice, which was essential to fully understanding the situation.'

In the next chapter we will look more closely at the debate around collaborative working and explore why a joint approach is, arguably, pertinent to all good practice in autism. However, we will examine why it is not always as efficient and effective as in the case study above.

References

Adamek, L., Nichols, S., Tetenbaum, S.P., Bregman, J., Pnzio, C.A. & Carr, E.G. (2011) Individual temperament and problem behaviour in children with ASD, *Focus on Autism and Other Developmental Disabilities*, 26/3, 173–183.

Chiang, H.-M. (2008) Expressive communication of children with autism: the use of challenging behaviour, *Journal of Intellectual Disability Research*, 52/11, 966–972.

Chung, K.M., Jung, W., Yang, J.W., Ben-Itzchak, E., Zachor, D.A., Furniss, F., Heyes, K., Matson, J.L., Kozlowski, A.M. & Barker, A.A. (2012) Cross cultural differences in challenging behaviours of children with ASD: An international examination between Israel, South Korea, U.K. and U.S.A., *Research in Autism Spectrum Disorders*, 6, 881–889.

Clements, J. & Zarkowska, E. (2000) *Behavioural Concerns & Autism Spectrum Disorders: Explanations and Strategies for Change*, London: Jessica Kingsley.

Durand, V.M., Hieneman, M., Clarke, S., Wang, M. & Rinaldi, M.L. (2013) Positive family intervention for severe challenging behaviour: a multisite randomised control trial, *Journal of Behavioural Interventions*, 15/3, 133–143.

Emerson, E. (2001) *Challenging Behaviour: Analysis and Intervention in People with Severe Intellectual Disabilities* (2nd edition), Cambridge: Cambridge University Press.

Holden, B. & Gitlesen, J.P. (2006) A total population study of challenging behaviour in the county of Hedmark, Norway: prevalence and risk markers, *Research in Developmental Disabilities*, 27, 456–465.

Horner, R.H. (2000) Positive behavior supports, *Focus on Autism and Other Developmental Disabilities*, 15, 97–105.

Horner, R.H., Dunlop, G., Koegel, R.L., Carr, E.G., Sailor, W., Anderson, J., Albin, R.W. & O'Neil, R.E. (1990) Toward a technology of 'nonaversive' behavioural support, *Journal of The Association for Persons with Severe Handicaps*, 15/3, 125–132.

Jang, J., Dixon, D.R., Tarbox, J. & Granpeesheh, D. (2011) Symptom severity and challenging behaviour in children with ASD, *Research in Autism Spectrum Disorders*, 5, 1028–1032.

Machalicek, W., O-Reilly, M.F., Beretvas, N., Sigafoos, J. & Lancioni, G.E. (2006) A review of interventions to reduce challenging behaviour in school settings for students with autism spectrum disorders, *Research in Autism Spectrum Disorders*, 1, 229–246.

Marshall, J.K. & Mirenda, P. (2002) Parent–professional collaboration for positive behaviour support in the home, *Focus on Autism and Other Developmental Disabilities*, 17/4, 216–228.

Matson, J.L., Mahan, S., Hess, J.A., Fodstad, J.C. & Neal, D. (2010) Progression of challenging behaviours in children and adolescents with ASDs as measured by the Autism Spectrum Disorders-Problem Behaviours for Children (ASD-PBC), *Research in Autism Spectrum Disorders*, 4, 400–404.

McClintock, K., Hall, S. & Oliver, C. (2003) Risk markers associated with challenging behaviours in people with intellectual disabilities: a meta-analytic study, *Journal of Intellectual Disability Research*, 47/6, 405–416.

McDonnell, A., Sturmey, P., Oliver, C., Cunningham, J., Hayes, S., Galvin, M., Walshe, C. & Cunningham, C. (2008) The effects of staff training on staff confidence and challenging behaviour in services for people with ASD, *Research in Autism Spectrum Disorders*, 2, 311–319.

McLean, B. & Grey, I. (2012) An evaluation of an intervention sequence outline in positive behaviour support for people with autism and severe escape-motivated challenging behaviour, *Journal of Intellectual and Developmental Disability*, 37/3, 209–220.

McTiernan, A., Leader, G., Healy, O. & Mannion, A. (2011) Analysis of risk factors and early predictors of challenging behaviour for children with autism spectrum disorder, *Research in Autism Spectrum Disorders*, 5, 1215–1222.

O'Neill, R., Horner, R., Albin, R., Sprague, J., Storey, K. & Newton, J.S. (1997) *Functional Assessment and Program Development for Problem Behavior: A Practical Handbook*, Pacific Grove, CA: Brooks/Cole.

Preece, D. (2014) Providing training in Positive Behaviour Support and Physical Interventions for parents of children with autism and related behavioural difficulties, *Support for Learning*, 29/2, 136–153.

Reece, M.R., Richman, D.M., Zarcone, J. & Zarcone, T. (2003) Individualising functional assessments for children with autism: the contribution of perseverative behavior and sensory disturbances to disruptive behavior, *Focus on Autism and Other Developmental Disabilities*, 18/2, 89–94.

Weiss, J.A., Cappadocia, M.C., MacMullin, J.A., Viecili, M. & Lunsky, Y. (2012) The impact of problem behaviour of children with ASD on parent mental health: the mediating role of acceptance and empowerment, *Autism*, 16/3, 261–274.

Whitaker, P. (2001) *Challenging Behaviour and Autism: Making Sense – Making Progress*, London, National Autistic Society.

Wolf, M. (1978) Social validity: the case for subjective measurement, or how behaviour analysis is finding its heart, *Journal of Applied Behaviour Analysis*, 11, 203–214.

Zarkowska, E. & Clements, J. (1994) *Problem Behaviour and People with Severe Learning Disabilities: The S.T.A.R. Approach* (2nd edition), London: Chapman and Hall.

Chapter 5

Autism and interprofessionalism

Interprofessionalism is now a recurring leitmotif in UK health, social care and education policy and legislation (OMYCA 2007, Scottish Government 2010, Health & Social Care Act 2012, DfE 2013, Scottish Government 2014). It is associated with imperatives to foster cross-service links by establishing habits of joint learning, knowledge transfer and exchange, and flexible working practices that enable shared responsibility for leadership, communication, assessment, planning, implementation and evaluation of service provision across service contexts. The aim of interprofessional working is ultimately to facilitate more efficient and effective provision, to enhance inclusion and to ensure improved social, health and educational outcomes for children, young people and adults.

For clients and the practitioners supporting them there is an inextricable link between effective autism provision and interprofessionalism. This is rooted in the long history of exclusion of individuals with autism across public services, which is associated in the research with a lack of staff training and joint working across services, and the widespread fragmentation of service provision (Ravet 2012). Together these factors constrain service responsiveness, limiting holism and undermining effectiveness. Evidence for this has been building steadily over the last four chapters and highlights the urgent need for a more widely shared understanding of autism, a joint discourse on autism and inclusion, and the development of consistent and coherent assessment approaches, interventions and behaviour support strategies that are based on the research and accurate use of the autism lens. Improving outcomes for individuals with autism is therefore strongly associated with improvements in autism training coupled with enhanced interprofessionalism. Arguably, interprofessionalism is the 'glue' required to bring cross-service unity. Achieving this, however, is likely to be highly challenging.

In chapter 5 we will explore the nature of this challenge by considering critically:

- the complexities of interprofessional working
- the role of interprofessional education (IPE) within autism training
- the impact of IPE on service provision

A case study will provide an example of impact in three service contexts and will illustrate the outcomes for workplace practice and clients with autism.

It should be noted that the term interprofessionalism tends to be used interchangeably in the literature with a number of other related terms such as multi-agency working, multidisciplinary working, joined-up working, partnership working and integrated working. There is little consensus as to the meaning of each of these terms (McCartney 2006). For the purposes of this chapter, the terms interprofessionalism or interprofessional working will be used when discussing working practices across service boundaries. The term collaboration is used to connote the process involved when professionals work cooperatively together within a service context.

Acknowledging the complexities of interprofessionalism

Though service unity is undoubtedly a fine aspiration, there is growing appreciation of the complexities of interprofessional working, and an understanding within the literature that effective interprofessional practice is not easily achieved (Carpenter & Dickinson 2008, Forbes & Watson 2009). Research has provided much evidence for this. For example, the barriers to interprofessionalism identified again and again in the literature include the impact of the clash of identities, cultures, values, roles, agendas, theoretical perspectives and discourses amongst professionals working at the boundaries between services (Forbes 2006, McCartney 2006, Edwards 2009). Inconsistencies across services in interpretations of the meaning of interprofessionalism have also been noted (HMIE 2006). These barriers clearly make the wholehearted pursuit of interprofessionalism difficult.

Imagine, for example, a scenario where a practitioner from health care works alongside a practitioner from social care to address the needs of a client with autism in a social care setting. Which practitioner should take the lead? How will their workloads and priorities be integrated? What if their working practices and expectations clash? How will differing perspectives, assessments and interventions be managed? There is clearly rich potential here for conflict unless there is a strong, shared culture of interprofessional working behind the practitioners, and a willingness to communicate, negotiate and compromise.

Another important strand of research explores qualitative distinctions between the various forms of interprofessionalism currently in operation across services. For example, Head (2003) distinguishes between superficial, shallow, purely functional interprofessional practice and an altogether more penetrating, deep and effective practice. The former tends to have a narrow focus on 'getting things done' and attending to specific issues and outcomes and is, perhaps, exemplified by the 'expert' or 'consultancy' model that continues to underpin much interprofessional working in the education sector, especially between teachers and speech and language therapists (Edwards 2009). Interprofessionalism in this context can be limited to a termly visit from the therapist, during which s/he conducts an assessment of a child's communication difficulties, develops strategies, provides a support plan and then simply passes it to the teacher with the expectation that it will be implemented prior to the next visit. Though there may have been some exchange of information in this scenario, and the learner with autism may make some progress, this is an example of 'getting things done' without any deep and meaningful interprofessional exchange. The outcomes are therefore likely to be limited and little joint professional development or joint learning will have taken place.

A deeper form of interprofessionalism aspires to joint development of shared understanding, values and vision, is more egalitarian and less hierarchical, and can be transformative for partners as well as the individuals they serve (Head 2003). Head associates it with personal and interprofessional learning that can lead to the development of genuine 'communities of support' and 'communities of learning' (Wenger 1998). In terms of the above scenario between a teacher and a speech and language therapist, a deeper and more genuine interprofessional partnership would involve joint assessment, planning, implementation and monitoring, and a more distributed form of leadership on the basis of negotiated and shared values, approaches and goals.

However, interprofessionalism of this quality can only be achieved with a certain amount of risk-taking. Explicit attention must be paid to the quality of communication and relationships within the interprofessional unit, and their underpinning power relations (Nixon 2009). 'Power with' rather than 'power over' relations that acknowledges the agency of partners and the value of their experience and contribution is essential to the development of good interprofessional practice (ibid.). Yet, it is often difficult for staff at the 'chalk-face' to address power imbalances in order to establish and maintain high-quality practice. Indeed, Edwards (2009) and Forbes (2006) propose that new power relations and creative joint initiatives cannot easily thrive in settings with traditional patterns of organisation, rigid bureaucracies and hierarchical structures. Thus, arguably, structural change must accompany professional change if we are to see real improvements in interprofessional practice. This is clearly a high demand requiring strategic planning at national and local service management level, as well as interprofessional level.

Interprofessional education and autism training

There are currently large and ever growing numbers of training opportunities in autism across the UK provided in the education, social care and health care sectors and by a plethora of independent training providers. These courses must guide students in navigating the complex medical, psychological and educational research literature in the field, in digesting autism theory, acquiring knowledge, skills and understanding of good practice, making links to relevant policy and legislation, and in applying and critically evaluating practice across service settings. However, many of these courses are uniprofessional (i.e. targeted at specific service groups, such as teachers, medical staff or social care workers, rather than mixed groups) and seek to explore autism within specific and narrow academic disciplines, research fields, service domains and workplace contexts. Other autism courses welcome a mix of professionals but do not explicitly provide opportunities for interprofessional learning and discussion of interprofessional issues and concerns.

Over the past decade interprofessional education (IPE) in autism has evolved as a way of addressing this gap. IPE is increasingly invoked within national educational and social policy (OECD 1998, HMIE 2002, Scottish Government 2008b, Scottish Government 2009), is now central to current thinking in the field of autism and a recurring theme within autism policy, literature and research (McKay & Dunlop 2004, Batten & Daly 2006, HMIE 2006, Scottish Government 2008a). A small number of postgraduate IPE programmes in autism have evolved in UK higher education institutions in response to this. Their structure and content reflects a determination to place interprofessionalism at the heart of advanced professional training and education in autism.

IPE occurs where 'two or more professions learn with, from and about each other' (WHO 2010). The central purpose is to provide joint opportunities for autism training whilst at the same time exploring the meaning of effective partnership across professions in order to improve service provision, facilitate service integration and enhance outcomes for service users:

> IPE is seen as a way to overcome ignorance and prejudice...By learning together, the professions will better understand each other and value what others bring to the practice of partnership.
> (Carpenter & Dickinson 2008, p. 1)

In order to facilitate interprofessional learning within autism training, a safe, dialogic space must be created for joint professional reflection and the sharing of working norms and practices. Learning opportunities and group tasks must be designed to invite direct exploration of the key barriers to autism and interprofessionalism within different service contexts. These opportunities should be embedded across courses, group activities and work-based assessments. The latter must explicitly reinforce expectations for meaningful interprofessionalism by requiring practitioners to plan autism interventions within an interprofessional, collaborative framework, to reflect critically upon the experience of interprofessionalism and critically evaluate the collaborative process alongside partners.

On the surface at least, IPE programmes like this have the potential to fulfil policy demands. They are generally welcomed as valuable additions to continuing professional development (CPD) provision and perceived as vital requisites for change within the field of autism and across service provision. It is hoped that IPE in autism will herald a new generation of well-informed and effective interprofessional practitioners.

However, an important question about IPE is whether this potential in translated into practice. Does it actually lead to real improvements in interprofessionalism amongst participants, and secure positive outcomes for service provision and individuals with autism? How can we know if IPE really works?

Does it work? Evaluating the impact of IPE in autism

If IPE works, it should have a positive impact on interprofessional working amongst the professionals who participate in it, and should result, in turn, in improvements in provision for clients with autism. In order to establish whether or not this is the case, it is necessary to undertake evaluative research that generates evidence of beneficial and sustained change.

Evaluative research might be defined as:

> the systematic application of social research procedures to assessing the conceptualisation, design, implementation and utility of social intervention programmes.
>
> (Freeth et al. 2005, p. 18)

The following case study provides an example of an IPE evaluation drawn from a wider research study into the efficacy of interprofessional development in autism (see Ravet 2011, Ravet 2012). The influence of the IPE programme on interprofessional practice, and the impact of practice change on service provision for clients with autism spectrum are highlighted. The findings are based on the perceptions of the practitioners who attended an IPE course, and also on the perceptions of their line managers and service funders.

However, before turning to the case study it ought to be noted that evaluative research based on participant perceptions is often criticised for generating a weak evidence base for effectiveness and impact (WHO 2010). It is claimed that participant self-report evaluations are highly subjective and that, as a result, causal links between practice and beneficial outcomes for clients cannot be easily evidenced (Carpenter & Dickinson 2008). Carpenter and Dickinson (2008) suggest that psychometric tools using standardised measures are essential to boost reliability and validity. Arguably, this may work well in large-scale, quantitative studies. However, it is only possible where outcomes are easily measureable and in outcome areas for which tools have been specifically developed and fully validated (ibid.). Variables, such as personality and environmental factors that might also influence outcomes, would have to be controlled. Thus, according to Barr et al. (1999) few studies 'dare' to claim direct causality, and those that do are considered 'highly suspect'.

Clearly, many outcomes of relevance and importance in this evaluative case study were not easily measureable; for example, how would you objectively measure increased practitioner confidence or enhanced client well-being? Thus, the researchers did not set out to make generalisable claims about outcomes but, rather, to explore participant perceptions of them, focusing largely on perceptions of changes in professional knowledge, understanding, skills and practice behaviour, and client responses to this in and across workplaces. The advantage of qualitative studies such as this is that the findings are well grounded in rich participant descriptions rather than in statistical outputs and researcher interpretations of data. However, to enhance reliability and strengthen the methodological rigour of the study, the practitioner perceptions were triangulated by line-manager and funder perceptions, and data collection was repeated several times – at the beginning, end and four months after the end of the IPE programme. (For a fuller discussion of these issues see Ravet 2012.)

Case study: IPE in autism

Ravet (2011/2012) researched student, line-manager and service-funder perceptions of the effectiveness and impact of a postgraduate IPE programme in Autism and Learning. The research was originally designed to establish whether autism theory and the interprofessional elements of the training were translated into practice, and to identify their impact on service provision and clients with autism. Only the interprofessional elements are reported here; the findings of the wider study are reported in Chapter 7.

The research was conducted as a small-scale interpretive study focusing on participant perceptions and using questionnaire and interview methods. It involved ten students from the education, health and voluntary sectors who all attended the postgraduate IPE certificate programme in Autism and Learning from September 2008– May 2009. Eight line managers responsible for overseeing the work of the students in their service contexts also contributed to the study. Three service officers responsible for selecting and funding the students also participated.

Findings

The findings of the evaluative study can be found in table 5.1. For reasons of space, only selective findings are presented in short, summary form. Direct quotes from research participants are included to illustrate and illuminate the findings.

Table 5.1 An evaluative case study of IPE in autism: outcomes relating to interprofessionalism

Changes in attitude and perception	*Facilitating factors:* • Clearer sense of professional role in relation to interprofessionalism • More aware of the constraints and working environments in other settings • More open to the views and perspectives of others • More aware of possibilities for networking/joint working • More confident and positive about working with others to enhance provision for clients with autism • More confident and positive about initiating organisational, structural, policy change, etc. in the workplace/across workplaces with others *'[IPE provided] a good opportunity to build networks of like-minded people...It has been useful to hear about the perspectives of others and the different issues they face. It helps us to think outside the box and challenge our reasoning for doing certain things.'* *Inhibiting factors:* • Logistics of interprofessional training • Argument that uniprofessional training may satisfy core business more effectively *'...We are always looking for interprofessional opportunities but, inevitably, we come back to our core business, which is single agency.'*
Acquisition of knowledge and skills	*Facilitating factors:* • Improved and updated knowledge and understanding of the value and role of interprofessionalism • Improved and updated knowledge and understanding of policy, legislation, literature and research relating to interprofessionalism • Greater knowledge and understanding of the roles and responsibilities of other professionals

Table 5.1 Continued

- Greater knowledge of how different services function
- Greater knowledge and understanding of the range of strategies and interventions used in other settings
- Greater awareness of service variations
- More holistic knowledge and understanding of autism services
- More skilful at identifying relevant agencies to collaborate with
- More confident about sharing ideas, information and participating in the collaborative process
- Learnt that it is important to 'learn from each other'
- Learnt that positive relationships are central to effective interprofessionalism
- Developed skills in planning joint projects and initiating change with others

'We all need to learn from each other – being from different agencies encourages sharing, consideration and appreciation of a more holistic viewpoint... [It also brings] insight into the constraints and the working environment... Relationships help with collaborative working.'

Inhibiting factors:
- Gaps in course regarding specific service approaches and provision

'Much of the content was aimed at school settings and may not have been as relevant to all on the course.'

Behavioural changes   **Facilitating factors:**
- Best practice shared more widely with colleagues
- Enhanced support for, and collaboration with, clients, parents, carers
- Enhanced interprofessionalism (except in education settings)
- More likely to initiate change at policy, practice, workplace and inter-agency level

'I spoke with other people from the Care sector and their attitude to autism was quite different...I was prompted to stretch the child more and to expect more of him...[so] I've been more persistent in my expectations and that's been really successful.'

Inhibiting factors:
- Lack of time for interprofessional collaboration (education contexts only)
- Lack of funding for wider staff IPE (education contexts only)

'I found working collaboratively with outside agencies a challenge in terms of being able to organise time to have a professional dialogue and to meet.'

Changes in organisational practice

Facilitating factors:
- Working towards better autism provision across services
- Working towards wider staff training
- Working towards more appropriate and effective planning and organisation of interprofessional working

'[The programme] has made me more aware of the fact that maybe we need to put an actual formal structure in place for collaborative work...[I] would like to do something like that in the future.'

Inhibiting factors:
- Structures and working practices inflexible (especially in education sector)

'Within the NHS you have more opportunities, perhaps, to be more interprofessional than, perhaps, in a discipline like Education. You can go and seek collaborative working as opposed to waiting for it to come to you.'

Perceived benefits to service users

- Wider, cross-service inclusion of clients with autism
- Needs met more effectively via higher-quality interprofessional support and intervention
- Greater consistency of support within and across services
- More opportunities for client/parent participation
- Improved client learning/well-being

'The person-centred planning approach...has had a huge influence on our [interprofessional] review meetings. We are using it a lot more across the school, not just with autistic children but with all children with special needs.'

Discussion

The findings above support the claim that IPE in autism in this particular higher education establishment improved attitudes to, and perceptions of, interprofessionalism and interprofessional roles, ensured the acquisition of relevant interprofessional knowledge and skills, and facilitated joint working across service boundaries and within the workplace (except in education contexts), which, in turn, enabled the students to positively influence wider workplace provision and improved outcomes for clients with autism. Other evaluative studies have identified similar benefits (Tate & Dunlop 2005, WHO 2010), though, so far, their numbers are few.

Though it is not possible to generalise from these small-scale findings, they are nonetheless indicative, and imply that much is to be gained from joint training and shared learning. IPE in autism therefore has the potential to play a central role in promoting better standards of provision for clients with autism.

However, the findings above also provide evidence of a number of inhibiting factors that acted as barriers to good interprofessional practice within this particular study.

A key finding was that some practitioners felt that issues relevant to autism and interprofessionalism in their own particular service were not covered in sufficient detail in the IPE programme, whilst issues relating to other service contexts were irrelevant to their own practice. This indicates the need for improvements in the balance of course inputs in this particular IPE programme. However, some researchers suggest that this is also a general problem for interprofessional education, as it cannot achieve the level of depth, detail and relevance that can be attained via uniprofessional training (Hall & Weaver 2001, Wood 2001).

Uniprofessional training is, by its very nature, fully responsive to the needs of practitioners in particular service settings. It can explore in detail the needs of clients with autism in these settings, and focus fully on the forms of provision required to address them. By contrast, practitioners on IPE programmes will explore autism theory in a generic way and then apply it, under guidance, to their own service context. The richness of this approach lies in the fact that the similarities and differences between the various ways that autism theory is applied across services can be shared and jointly analysed. This enables practitioners to gain insights into the strengths and limitations of different forms of provision; insights that will be invaluable as they work across service boundaries to bridge service gaps. Current policy and legislations now requires this.

However, some practitioners may need support to see the powerful, though indirect, relevance of this sort of sharing. Thus, though superficially IPE does not appear to address their core business, arguably it is nonetheless highly pertinent to the development of interprofessional awareness, and

ensures a knowledge and understanding of cross-service issues. More evaluative research of interprofessional training may be required to establish whether this problem is widespread, and how it might be addressed, for it has implications for the future of interprofessional training. Clearly, it is vital that practitioners see the value of listening to others and learning from them. Since this is an attitude central to the success of interprofessional working, it may be helpful to embed explicit discussion of it in IPE courses, rather than taking its development as self-evident and inevitable. The study was helpful in surfacing this problem.

Various other factors that inhibited the implementation of good interprofessional practice amongst the students in the study were highlighted in the findings, such as time, workloads, lack of funding for IPE, and inflexible working practices and structures. However, this was true only for the education contexts in the study, not for the health and social care contexts. The education funders interviewed concurred with the students that interprofessionalism was limited in the schools under consideration. One said: 'With regard to other professionals, I can't say that I am aware of [joint working].' Another funder suggested that this lack of interprofessionalism was possibly historical but suggested that the culture is beginning to change as policy on integrated working takes hold. He was hopeful that IPE in autism might help to stimulate this culture shift and encourage better uptake of interprofessional practice.

However, factors that inhibit interprofessionalism, such as those listed above, should be of serious concern to all those with a stake in improving autism services, for they diminish returns on investment in staff training by reducing its impact on workplace and client outcomes. They are therefore a drain on both energy and financial resources. How should this be addressed?

This question will be discussed in more detail in chapter 7 when we consider the problem of the implementation gap and how to bridge it.

Conclusion

We have now entered an era in which IPE is being hailed as an innovative educational approach that could revolutionise traditional practices and service delivery, bringing about a transformation of service culture (WHO 2010). Indeed, interprofessionalism is now regarded as central to the provision of high-quality, integrated services for individuals with autism, and is widely advocated.

The case study discussed above appears to confirm the legitimacy of some of these claims and clarifies the specific benefits that IPE can bring to practitioners and the children, young people and adults with autism whom they serve. However, we must bear in mind the methodological minefield mentioned earlier in relation to evaluative research. We should be very cautious about making strong, dogmatic claims about the link between interprofessionalism and improved outcomes for service users on the basis of small-scale qualitative studies such as the one presented above (Coe 2009).

What we urgently need is more high-quality evaluative IPE research that can provide rigorous evidence of positive outcomes. We also need decision-makers at national policy level who value such research, are willing to fund it and who grasp the importance of drawing on it to provide robust evidence for policy claims (Coe 2009).

In the next chapter we will analyse how interprofessionalism, and all of the key issues addressed so far in this book, are connected to, and encapsulated by, the notion of the 'autism friendly workplace'. We will explore how practitioners can draw on formal and informal practice audits and evaluations to monitor workplace practice, identify and reduce the factors that inhibit service development, and plan strategically for workplace improvement.

References

Barr, H., Hammick, M., Freeth, D., Koppel, I. & Reeves, S. (1999) Evaluating interprofessional education: two systematic reviews for health & social care, *British Educational Research Journal*, 25, 533–544.

Batten, A. & Daly, J. (2006) *Make School Make Sense: Autism & Education in Scotland – The Reality for Families*, London: National Autistic Society.

Carpenter, J. & Dickinson, H. (2008) *Interprofessional Education & Training*, Bristol: Policy Press.

Coe, R. (2009) School improvement: reality & illusion, *British Journal of Educational Studies*, 57/4, 363–379.

DfE (Department for Education) (2013) *Working Together to Safeguard Children*, London: DfE.

Edwards, A. (2009) Understanding boundaries in inter-professional work, *Scottish Educational Review*, 41/1, 5–19.

Forbes, J. (2006) For social justice & inclusion: engaging with the other, *Journal of Research in Special Educational Needs*, 6/2, 99–107.

Forbes, J. & Watson, C. (2009) *Service Integration in Schools: Research & Policy Discourses, Practices & Future Prospects*, Rotterdam: Sense Publications.

Freeth, D., Reeves, S., Koppel, I., Hammick, M. & Barr. H. (2005) *Evaluating Interprofessional Education: A Self-Help Guide*. Accessible: www.health. heacademy.ac.uk/publications/occasionalpaper/occp5 (accessed Sept. 2010).

Hall, P. & Weaver, L. (2001) Interdisciplinary education and teamwork: a long and winding road, *Medical Education*, 35/9, 867–875.

Head, G. (2003) Effective collaboration: deep collaboration as an essential element of the learning process, *Journal of Educational Inquiry*, 4/2, 47–62.

Health and Social Care Act (2012) London: The Stationery Office.

HMIE (2002) *Count Us In: Achieving Inclusion in Scottish Schools*, Edinburgh: Scottish Executive Education Department.

HMIE (2006) *Education for Pupils with Autism Spectrum Disorders*, Livingston: HMIE.

McCartney, E. (2006) Interprofessional & Interagency Working (Paper 14), *The Research & Policy Discourses of Service Integration: ESRC Seminar 1 proceedings*, Aberdeen: University of Aberdeen.

McKay, T.A.W.N. & Dunlop, A.W.A. (2004) *The Development of a National Training Framework for Autistic Spectrum Disorders: A Study of Training for Professionals Working in the Field of ASD in Scotland*, London: National Autistic Society.

Nixon, J. (2009) The conditions for interprofessional learning: the centrality of relationships, in J. Forbes & C. Watson (eds), *Service Integration in Schools: Research & Policy Discourses, Practices & Future Prospects*, Rotterdam: Sense Publications, 167–181.

OECD (Organisation for Economic Co-operation and Development) (1998) *Coordinating Services for Children and Youth At Risk: A World View*, Paris: OECD.

OMYCA (Office of the Minister for Children and Youth Affairs) (2007) *The Agenda for Children's Services: A Policy Handbook*, Dublin: The Stationery Office.

Ravet, J. (2011) Interprofessional training in autism: impact on professional development and workplace practice, *Good Autism Practice*, 12/1, 79–87.

Ravet, J. (2012) From interprofessional education to interprofessional practice: exploring the implementation gap, *Professional Development in Education*, 38/1, 49–64.

Scottish Government (2008a) *Commissioning Services for People on the Autism Spectrum: Policy & Practice Guidance*, Edinburgh: Scottish Government. Accessible: www.scotland.gov.uk (accessed Aug. 2010).

Scottish Government (2008b) *A Guide to Getting It Right For Every Child (GIRFEC)*. Accessible: www.scotland.gov.uk (accessed Aug. 2010).

Scottish Government (2009) *The Autism Toolbox: An Autism Resource for Scottish Schools*, Edinburgh: Scottish Government.

Scottish Government (2010) *Guidance on Partnership Working between Allied Health Professionals and Education*, Edinburgh: Scottish Government.

Scottish Government (2014) Public Bodies (Joint Working) (Scotland) Act 2014, Edinburgh: Scottish Government.

Tate, C. & Dunlop, A.W.A. (2005) The impact of training on practice: insights from postgraduate study of autism. ISEC Conference 2005, Glasgow.

Wenger, E. (1998) *Communities of Practice: Learning, Meaning and Identity*, Cambridge: Cambridge University Press.

Wood, D.F. (2001) Interprofessional education: still more questions than answers, *Medical Education*, 35/9, 816–817.

World Health Organisation (WHO) (2010) *Framework for Action on Interprofessional Education & Collaborative Practice*. Accessible: www.who.int/hrh/nursing_midwifery/en (accessed Aug. 2010).

Chapter 6

Strategic planning for autism friendly services

In the autism literature, the notion of the 'autism friendly environment' is widely discussed and positively correlated to enhanced quality of life for individuals with autism (Billstedt et al. 2011). Individuals themselves, their families and professionals increasingly refer to contexts, events, resources and practices that are 'autism friendly'. Indeed, the term has fallen into common usage and suggests the existence of a set of adaptations that make it possible for people with autism to feel at ease, participate and thrive in different environments. It is therefore an umbrella term with a range of possible dimensions.

This chapter will briefly discuss the characteristics of the autism friendly service environment then explore, in more detail, how this might be planned for, developed and evaluated to establish and maintain high-quality standards. I will define the autism friendly environment as a service context in which the physical, sensory, social, communication, learning and organisational environments have been purposefully modified, using the autism lens, in order to maximise the inclusion and well-being of individuals with autism. Note, once again, that by 'learning environment' I mean any environment in which life-long learning needs are assessed, learning purposes are formulated, knowledge is imparted, skills are taught, tasks are issued, and so forth. So this might be in a classroom, therapy unit, daycare centre or home – anywhere in which people with autism are supported by practitioners with particular academic, social or therapeutic learning goals in mind.

Arguably, the desire to achieve 'autism friendly' status should be a priority for all professionals in any workplace setting, since we currently live in a policy and legislative context driven by inclusive values and expectations of social justice and equality (see chapter 1). For example, the recent Equality Act (2010) seeks to advance the rights of individuals and ensure equality of opportunity for all. Under this Act, public sector authorities have a legal duty to:

- eradicate discrimination
- proactively promote equality of opportunity
- foster good relations across relevant protected characteristics (e.g. disability)

The intention is to prevent discrimination happening in the first place by changing the culture of public authorities so that they think about, and take action on, equality as part of their mainstream business.

(NHS Health Scotland 2011, appendix 5, p. 2)

The autism friendly environment might be viewed as the logical outcome of the enactment of this legal duty since it is the antithesis of the discriminatory environment. However, discrimination rights can only be protected, and inclusion ensured, where good practice is fully and effectively enacted. Hence the emphasis in the Equality Act on the importance of public sector authorities and professionals working *proactively* in pursuit of anti-discrimination practices, taking wholehearted responsibility for them. This means creating a fully accessible and responsive context which is maximally adapted to clients with autism, rather than passing the burden of responsibility for adaptation to the clients themselves (Billstedt et al. 2011). This distinction is absolutely pivotal but is still not widely appreciated (Ravet 2011).

In this chapter we will undertake a critical analysis of how professionals might set about establishing an autism friendly environment by considering the characteristics associated with it and the strategic planning process required to achieve 'autism friendly' status. A case study will then be presented to exemplify this.

The autism friendly environment: key characteristics

The need for strategic planning across autism services has been increasingly recognised over the past decade (NIASA 2003). This accounts for the development of autism strategies, policy and legislation at national level across the UK (see chapter 1). It also explains the proliferation of good practice guidance and accreditation programmes at regional and local service level that have been designed to clarify the characteristics of the autism friendly environment and promote self-evaluation processes as a basis for service improvement. Much of this guidance is service specific and relates, for example, to education (e.g. DfES 2002, AET 2011), health and social care (Scottish Government 2008) or assessment and diagnostic services (SIGN 2007). The National Autistic Society, on the other hand, provides a general autism accreditation service that offers a 'unified standard of excellence and a systematic framework for continuous self-examination and development' suitable to a wide range of local authority services (see www.autism.org.uk).

Most of the standards used in these good practice guidance documents are based on expert opinion in consultation with stakeholder groups, with particular emphasis on the participation of clients with autism. Though they may vary slightly in their details depending on authorship and the context focus, what they all have in common, as we shall see below, is a set of criteria that pinpoint the standards for good practice.

The purpose of the criteria is to provide an objective, base-line standard against which different facets of service provision can be evaluated. The assessment process then provides a detailed and structured set of goals towards which everyone can strive. They enable management and practitioners to identify, acknowledge and celebrate existing good practice, whilst working towards improvement in clearly targeted areas of weakness and service gaps. The result, in theory at least, should be evidence-based service improvement, with clients with autism as key participants and foremost beneficiaries (Scottish Government 2008).

For the purposes of this book, the following criteria from the National Autistic Society accreditation programme are used to define the general characteristics of the autism friendly environment. These criteria have been selected because they are relevant to any context and will therefore have significance for readers practising in a range of service settings. The NAS accreditation programme is used widely in Britain and is associated with high standards of excellence. Indeed, their criteria are referred to in much of the service-specific good practice guidance explored later.

The criteria are:

- a specialised knowledge and understanding of autism
- the knowledge and understanding of autism consistently informs the organisation, the resources and management of the organisation
- the knowledge and understanding of autism consistently informs the assessment and support plan for people who use the service
- the knowledge and understanding of autism consistently informs all aspects of practice

Training issues

It should not be surprising that specialist knowledge of autism is the first and fundamental requirement for the development of the autism friendly workplace. The importance of a sound knowledge and understanding of the condition amongst front-line staff has been repeatedly emphasised in the early chapters of this book, as it enables practitioners to form the 'autism lens' through which they can make sense of the behaviour and responses of clients and develop appropriate interventions to meet their needs. These issues have been examined in depth (see chapters 2, 3, 4 and 5).

However, apart from front-line staff, it is also important that management staff have autism training, since they must be able to anticipate the impact of the organisational structures, processes, environment and resources upon clients with autism, and make executive decisions about appropriate adaptations across the workplace to ensure consistency and coherence. Yet training for this group is often overlooked, creating considerable problems for staff and clients (Ravet 2012).

For example, when school management staff are untrained, they are less likely to encourage curriculum and pedagogical innovations to meet the needs of pupils with autism, or support teacher decisions about pupil behaviour – especially where these challenge accepted norms (ibid.). In a social care context, staff are now widely expected to provide support for personal care during strictly timed 15-minute home visits (LCD 2013). Untrained management staff may fail to appreciate the extra time needed to individualise support for clients with autism and to create an unhurried, low-arousal context that fosters participation and independence. This requires some flexibility in the organisation of support, which, in turn, relies on management insight and a realistic appraisal of the situation. Management training is therefore essential.

The autism research literature repeatedly emphasises that the essential pre-requisite for meeting the requirement for autism knowledge and understanding across education, health, social care and the voluntary sector is the widespread availability of autism education and training. This must be available at a range of levels to suit a range of staff development needs, from basic autism awareness through to advanced specialist knowledge (MacKay & Dunlop 2004, Batten & Daly 2006). Currently, however, there is a problem with training provision at both national and local levels across the UK (Department of Health 2010, Scottish Government 2011).

This situation has arisen partly because the identification of autism, and the demand for services, has far outpaced the development and uptake of training provision, with the result that there are many front-line staff supporting children, young people and adults with autism in the UK, who still lack the basic knowledge, understanding and skills to do so (McKay & Dunlop 2004). The outcome is low standards leading to discriminatory practices and exclusion.

Another problem is that training is currently undertaken, at both national and local levels, in an uncoordinated way and on an ad-hoc basis, by a range of different providers from the charitable sector, further and higher education sectors and from local trainers within education, health and social care services. What is currently lacking is overarching planning and coordination of training (Ravet 2012). The result is a 'patchwork' of provision of uneven and unreliable quality, with wildly varying opportunities for training progression and development.

In their landmark study of 1500 practitioners, service providers, training providers and parents in Scotland, McKay and Dunlop (2004) uncovered 'major gaps in training at every level across every sector' (p. 3). They went on to comment:

For most practitioners there is no pre-service training even at awareness raising level, and most in-service training is only introductory, even for those whose work is mainly in the ASD field.

(p. 3)

Unfortunately, despite evidence of some improvement in certain areas, the situation described by McKay and Dunlop in 2004 still largely prevails in Scotland (Scottish Government 2011) and elsewhere in the UK. Training in autism awareness therefore remains high on recent UK national strategy agendas. Indeed, within the Scottish strategy, two out of ten best practice indicators focus on training:

2   Access to training and development to inform staff and improve understanding amongst professionals about ASD.
4   An ASD Training Plan to improve the knowledge and skills of those who work with people with ASD, to ensure that people with ASD are properly supported by trained staff.

(ibid. p. 12)

The second point is linked to a key recommendation to repeat McKay and Dunlop's national audit of training provision and to develop a national training framework that will organise, structure and coordinate autism training across Scotland (ibid. p. 15). This initiative, should it come about, will significantly improve the national training picture and, by extension, overall standards of autism friendly practice and provision. This is summed up in the Scottish Government vision statement:

Our vision is that individuals on the autism spectrum ... have confidence in their services to treat them fairly so that they are able to have meaningful and satisfying lives.

(Scottish Government 2011, p. 6)

Whilst this vision is laudable, it is pertinent to ask when this promise of 'fair treatment' is likely to be fulfilled. In Scotland, this will surely depend on how quickly a national training framework can be organised and operationalised, and when and how quickly and effectively trained practitioners can translate their knowledge, skills and understanding into high-quality inclusive practice. This will not be an overnight process. However, strategic thinking at national level will, potentially at least, help to ensure that it is a planned process.

The importance of leadership and distributed leadership

However, the process of change in autism services need not only flow down from government thinkers to regional leaders, to service managers, to front-line practitioners, and thence to clients with autism, though this form of top-down leadership clearly has an important place. On the contrary, strategic planning at workplace level, undertaken by front-line staff, can make a vital contribution to change by feeding into national planning from the bottom up (Ravet 2012). By 'workplace' I mean an individual service unit such as a specific school, clinic, therapy unit or care home. For strategic planning at this level to be effective, however, staff must first feel confident about showing leadership, being pro-active and participating in workplace decision-making processes. Thus, we are talking, here, about the potential of 'distributed leadership' rather than traditional notions of leadership in the workplace.

The latter is associated with a set of qualities, attributes and skills solely accredited to specific individuals, usually senior members of staff, who are officially awarded a leadership and decision-making remit. By contrast, the notion of distributed leadership suggests the possibility that these qualities, attributes and skills can be developed by all members of staff at any level of a workplace structure, and embraces the idea of networks of individuals working together for change (Timperley 2005). This understanding of leadership has become increasingly popular amongst policy makers since the 1990s and is now widely claimed across service settings (ibid.). However, the reality belies the rhetoric in many cases, since the definition of distributed leadership varies considerably and its effectiveness depends on a range of internal and external variables (ibid.). For example, in some workplaces, for socio-cultural and historical reasons, staff are given only limited opportunities to show leadership and/or limited agency, autonomy or control to influence workplace practice. Distributed leadership can therefore be superficial and tokenistic in these contexts (ORO 2003) or lead to incoherence, incompetent and ineffective reform (Timperley 2005). However, where there is strong commitment to the principle of distributed leadership amongst management, and greater fluidity within the ethos and organisational structures of the workplace, it is possible for practitioners to group together in different formations for different purposes to initiate and sustain collaborative change (ibid.).

Our concern, in the next section, is with strategic planning within this model of distributed leadership. What contribution can practitioners make to the quest for the autism friendly workplace?

The strategic planning process

Strategic planning might be defined as a process of determining a future direction, identifying associated goals, and allocating resources to pursue this direction in a planned way. Practitioners have a central role to play in this process.

Workplace auditing

In order to set the wheels of strategic planning in motion, the first step in any workplace context must be honest, thorough and detailed 'auditing'. Auditing is generally understood as a systematic, independent, criterion-driven and evidence-based process that results in an audit report. Auditing asks both:

- how are we doing? and
- how do we know?

To answer these questions the auditing process involves:

- collaborative **self-evaluation** involving the use of standards ratings
- identification of **evidence** (documentary, observational or verbal) as proof of ratings

Let us examine this auditing process in more detail.

How are we doing and how do we know?

At first glance, these are simple and straightforward questions. Clearly, they call for some form of data collection within the workplace about the state of current practice, with some way of proving that claims are valid, and some way of rating this practice against specific criteria regarding the autism friendly workplace. It begs four further questions:

- What auditing tools will be used?
- What evidence will be rallied?
- What standards ratings will be adopted?
- Who will be involved?

As mentioned at the beginning of this chapter, there are a wide range of auditing tools available to services, some of which are 'in-house' and specific, and others of which are generic. Clearly, the auditing tools must be fit for purpose and address the issue of the autism friendly environment in a way that is relevant and appropriate to the service context. However, whatever form they take, they must address the fundamental generic accreditation criteria listed above.

For example, the extract from a speech and language therapy auditing tool (DfES 2002) reproduced in box 6.1 reflects the focus and priorities of this particular service. The tool provides a list of questions about service provision that requires practitioners to systematically reflect upon, and evaluate, all aspects of current practice.

Box 6.1: Extract from Speech & Language Therapy Auditing Tool

Pointer	Evidence	Implementation level	Progress/comments
1. Does the speech and language therapist have either specialist knowledge of ASDs or have access to support and guidance from a therapist or other professional specialising in ASDs?	There is a system of accreditation for SLTs working with specialisms including ASDs. There are clear systems of support from experienced and knowledgeable SLTs for SLTs working with children with ASDs. An ASD Special Interest Group exists where professionals can share knowledge and good practice.	Levels: school and local authority	☐ Rating
2. Is the speech and language therapist's assessment broad based, co-ordinated and integrated?	Assessment takes into account all aspects of communication and social functioning, not just speech and language. The assessment is part of a co-ordinated multi-disciplinary assessment which considers how aspects of the assessment relate to and influence one another. SLTs use assessment tools that are sensitive enough to identify and address the needs of children with Asperger's Syndrome.	Level: school	☐ Rating

(DfES 2002, p. 104)

The sort of evidence required to substantiate claims is specifically indicated in this document in order to steer the auditing process in the right direction. The quality of this evidence matters a great deal. For example, in response to the first item about specialist knowledge and guidance, it would not be sufficient to simply state that all staff must attend a one-day training course or have access to the Internet where they can find more out about autism for themselves. Rather, what is required is clear evidence that the service has a well-documented and systematic approach to supporting staff development in autism, that can be independently verified via staff testimony and/or confirmed via observation. Thus if, as the document proposes, the service has a system of accreditation that provides advanced training, runs a mentoring scheme to support staff development, and has a Specialist Interest Group where practitioners can share good practice, then the service can reasonably claim to have strong evidence for the achievement of this item. Clearly, evidence must be robust if it is to be convincing and form the basis for future planning.

This evidence is related to another important feature of the auditing tool: the rating system. In the case of the speech and language therapy auditing tool, auditors are asked to rate practice and provision using a four-point rating scale where 1 represents items which have not been achieved and for which there is no current evidence, 2 indicates that there is some, but not sufficient, evidence of an item being achieved, 3 indicates that an item is well catered for and requires only a little further development, and 4 represents items which have been successfully achieved and for which there is good provision and a range of evidence. Since, logically, judgments about rating are inextricably linked to evidence, then no evidence, or weak evidence, must correlate to low ratings and vice versa.

This may all seem like simple common sense. However, auditing can easily lapse into a superficial, 'tick-box' procedure conducted without critical reflection upon the meaning of the process and with scant regard for reality. It hardly bears mention that this approach simply leads nowhere. By contrast, a full, honest and searching collaborative audit can be immensely illuminating for all involved. It will shine a light on areas of strength as well as gaps and areas of weakness, and provide a valid and reliable basis for future service planning and development.

For this reason, it is vital that judgments about evidence and ratings are not solely provider-driven but involve a range of stakeholders including clients with autism and their families. This is because notions of 'achievement' and judgements about 'evidence' can be highly subjective and depend on one's role and priorities. So, for example, a service user may have a very different sense of the effectiveness of a particular aspect of practice than a service manager who is not on the receiving end of service provision (DfE 2002). Auditing must therefore be well grounded in the real-life experiences of management, staff, collaborative partners *and* service users if the outcomes are to be meaningful, credible and useful. To facilitate this, careful thought for the design of service-user questionnaires and interviews is necessary so that communication barriers can be overcome, and participation enabled. Ethically, it is vital, wherever possible, that participation is anonymous and confidential so that honest challenges to practice can be confidently made without fear of detrimental personal or professional consequences.

Action planning: what do we do next?

Auditing should result in a range of data highlighting those aspects of practice and provision that are effective and those aspects that are weak or lacking and need to be addressed. Since the *'raison d'être'* of auditing is service improvement, the next step is to decide exactly what must be improved and how this will be operationalised. Further strategic thinking is required here.

Firstly, it is important to identify priority targets, especially in cases where a number of service gaps and weaknesses have been identified through auditing. There may not be capacity, in terms of staffing, resources, time and funding, to address all these issues at once. Thus, prioritising is vital in order to deal, in the first instance, with issues fundamental to the progress of the overall strategic plan. Again, people's sense of priorities will vary depending on their position and role. Strategic thinking must therefore be undertaken collaboratively so that ownership of, and responsibility and accountability for, priority targets can be fully shared. This is more likely to ensure the longevity and sustainability of the change process (Villa & Thousand 2005).

Box 6.2 provides an exemplar of an action plan, based on a speech and language service audit, that indicates how the action planning process can be documented and operationalised. Here, one priority target is listed, and plans, timelines and 'success criteria' specified. The success criteria are the outcomes that will enable staff, clients and strategic planners to recognise when the target has been achieved. They are an important feature of the document because they require planners to think through the process in detail to identify what success might actually look like. This encourages thorough, realistic and holistic thinking, and avoids the temptation to set lots of targets but neglect the important question of their desired impact.

Planners must then consider how each target will be implemented, the training and resources it will require, the interprofessional working it will involve, and who will take responsibility for overall leadership. For implementation, it is vital to adopt the autism lens and draw on practical, evidence-based strategies and interventions such as those presented in chapter 3. This should be undertaken collaboratively, in line with national policy and good autism practice, in order to widen ownership, share resources and training, and maximise consistency and coherence. A completion date for implementation is vital since it forces planners to ensure that the time line of the project is achievable within the constraints of the organisational agenda.

Box 6.2: Exemplar action plan based on Speech & Language Therapy Audit

Target	Collaborative partners/resources	Plans and timelines	Date/duration/responsibilities	Success criteria
Enhance staff training in autism across the therapy unit	**Collaborators:** Autism specialists within local and regional teams NAS trainers and other local specialist trainers Higher education establishments (for award-bearing autism programmes) 'Critical Friends' form related services **Resources:** Funding Support from Human Resources	Establish 'critical friend' group from all related services to support and guide implementation (within one month of start) Provide autism training at a range of levels: • Awareness – for all staff (by end of year 1) • Basic – for all front-line therapists (by end of year 1) • Advanced – for all managers and for therapists working directly with children with autism (by end of year 2) • Advanced award-bearing (i.e. postgraduate certificate level and above) – for specialist therapists (by end of year 3) Set up a training database to record staff training needs, training levels and completed training programmes (by end of year 1) Organise peer support teams (by end of year 1) Organise regular meetings to review and update practice (by end of year 2)	Starting now 3-year rolling programme Senior service manager in lead role but planning and organisation distributed and collaborative All staff to participate and initiate	By end of year 1: • all staff working at awareness or basic level of training as appropriate • database fully functioning and effective • regular peer support, autism practice and special interest group meetings • all staff participating in, and taking responsibility for, action planning • distributed leadership model in operation • autism practice is improved and staff are confident • service for children with autism is improved, and children, parents and schools are benefiting By end of year 2: • as above • all managers and front-line therapists working at advanced training level

Box 6.2: Continued

Target	Collaborative partners/ resources	Plans and timelines	Date/duration/ responsibilities	Success criteria
		Identify two specialist therapists and document their roles and responsibilities, e.g. for in-house awareness training (by end of year 2)		• specialist therapists will have achieved their award-bearing status
		Organise ASC special interest group (by end of year 2)		By the end of year 3: • as above • two autism specialists are undertaking their roles and responsibilities as documented
		Monitor outcomes for schools, children with autism and parents using a simple online survey and interview process (at end of year 3)		• all staff are working with an appropriate level of autism knowledge and understanding

Evaluation (what evidence is needed? who will participate? when?, etc.)
Evidence: management, staff and client evaluation sheets, database evidence, group interview data, critical friend and collaborative partner feedback.
Who: management, staff, clients (including children wherever possible), critical friends and other collaborative partners.
When: mini review at end of years 1 and 2; major audit and review at end of year 3.

Evaluation and review

Of course, the success of the strategic process cannot simply be assumed just because auditing, action planning and implementation have taken place. Thus, an equally important section of the document focuses on the 'evaluation strategy' needed to check the effectiveness of new developments, and their stability and robustness over time. This is likely to involve regular staff monitoring and review, and the periodic gathering of client feedback and evaluation.

This can either be done by creating simple questionnaires that request staff or client views on the outcomes of the implementation, or by engaging in direct dialogue with them about it. The former is more effective with large numbers of people. The latter can yield rich information but is only practical where numbers are small. Responses from questionnaires and/or interviews can then be collated and analysed to identify successful outcomes and, importantly, to pinpoint areas requiring further refinement.

By the end of the strategic planning process, autism provision in any context should be on a planned trajectory towards 'autism friendly' status. This is an ongoing, iterative process that must be continuously reflective and analytical of workplace practice, but also responsive to internal developments such as staffing, funding and resource fluctuations, and external developments such as new autism research findings, policy shifts and the changing needs of clients.

In some service contexts, a formal external inspection process periodically occurs. This might be undertaken by a national body commissioned by the government, such as the Care Quality Commission (CQC) in Social Care and the Health Care Service, or Her Majesty's Inspectorate (HMI) in the education service. Their purpose is to check quality standards through an independent auditing process similar to the one outlined above. Clearly, the outcomes of internal and independent external auditing should be linked and considered complementary.

The following case study illustrates the auditing and action planning process in operation in a residential care context.

Case study

This case study provides an example of how one practitioner attempted to enhance the quality of autism friendly service provision in her context, not just by enhancing and developing her own practice, but by seizing an opportunity to show leadership and initiate an intervention to enhance practice amongst her colleagues. It therefore illustrates how auditing, target setting and collaborative action planning, within a context of distributed leadership, can work very effectively to bring about service improvement from the bottom up, rather than from the top down.

Enhancing choice and independence in a residential school

Sarah is an experienced member of staff who works and lives in a Camphill residential school for children and young adults with complex additional needs. She supports four students with a diagnosis of autism and also supervises new members of the staffing team.

Audit and target-setting

Practice in this residential school is informed, amongst other influences, by the values, expectations and good practice guidance set out in National Care Standards for Scotland (NCS undated) and by the National Autistic Society in the Autism Accreditation Programme (NAS undated). The school had recently been inspected and accredited by both of these organisations when Sarah started her internal audit of the autism friendly workplace. It was therefore appropriate for Sarah to draw on their reports as a source of comprehensive data to inform her own analysis.

Both reports highlighted many areas of 'very good' practice across the school where the assessment criteria had been met. However, the autism accreditation report highlighted a significant weakness in provision:

> [F]requent use was being made of verbal or physical prompts to instruct and support young people with autism creating and perpetuating a reliance on 1:1 adult intervention.

The report advised that staff should receive support and training in strategies to reduce this prompt-dependency.

In response to the above, and in collaboration with others, Sarah decided to focus action planning upon the following priority target arising from the audit:

• to promote client choice and independence in daily life by reducing prompt dependency.

Action planning and implementation

Sarah wished to develop a joint response to this target and was keen to involve staff in action planning and intervention, rather than simply imposing change on them. She did not, therefore, proceed by requesting training from management or from an outside agency. Instead, in order to facilitate change, Sarah wanted to model the concept of 'distributed leadership' in her workplace context. Sarah felt that this notion would sit well within the workplace culture where staff were regularly given time and space for supervision and discussion. She wished to draw on the knowledge and understanding of autism she had recently gained during a course of postgraduate study to support the development of her peers. With the permission of her line manager she therefore proceeded as follows:

- Using a short open-ended questionnaire, she began by critically exploring practice relating to student choice and independence with a group of 12 co-workers to establish their motivation and aims. Here Sarah discovered that, for many of the co-workers, theoretical knowledge of autism played little or no role in informing their everyday practice. This accounted for their reliance on traditional verbal and physical prompts, and their lack of awareness of the problem of prompt-dependency this can generate. They also seemed unaware of the value and efficacy of a visual approach.
- Sarah followed this up with informal interviews with co-workers, which aimed to explore more fully their responses to the questionnaire and their current approach to promoting choice and independence. Here she found that even the more experienced co-workers with some theoretical knowledge of autism had difficulties building the bridge between theory and practice. In other words, they did not know how to *apply* their knowledge of autism to meet client needs, with the result that they defaulted to traditional, generic approaches that were not autism friendly.
- Finally, Sarah asked the co-workers to consider what form of support might enable them to address these issues. Collaboratively, it was established that the co-workers needed support for professional development through autism training involving a mixture of interactive group work and direct teaching.

The outcomes of these discussions formed the basis of a training session on the theme 'promoting independence and choice'.

Sarah therefore pursued her priority target via a training workshop. The specific purpose of the workshop was to address gaps in staff knowledge and understanding of autism theory – especially explanatory psychological theories relating to weak theory of mind, central coherence and executive functioning – that might support their understanding of student behaviour. Sarah then explored the practical applications of these theories and used case studies to help the co-workers to apply theory to practice in order to develop a strong autism lens. She felt that this knowledge and understanding would enable staff to analyse student support needs more deeply, explain them more fully and help them to develop individualised, structured and visual interventions to address them. This, in turn, would reduce reliance on undifferentiated verbal and physical prompts. Sarah hoped that this training would help staff to be more analytical, pro-active and effective.

Evaluation and review

Feedback from the co-workers, gained via a short questionnaire, was 'very positive'. The co-workers indicated that the theoretical review had been highly valuable. Indeed, one co-worker commented: 'The psychological theories were new to me and I found them very interesting.' Another commented: 'It was helpful to look at the theories and to relate them to choice and independence.' The co-workers found the case studies especially helpful in enabling them to reflect upon practice in the light of theory and challenge their understanding of client behaviour. One commented: '...we talked a lot about practice – which was very helpful. Also, the theories are interesting when you connect them to your practice.' Much 'lively discussion' was generated by the case studies.

The co-workers' evaluations indicated that, by the end of the training, they felt they were in a better position to draw on and apply their knowledge and understanding of autism to reduce verbal and physical prompts and enhance choice and independence through the use of visual supports. Co-workers stated that the training had helped them to 'go deeper' in their analysis of client needs and had given them a 'refreshed view' of good autism practice. Others stated that they would now be able to 'assess what I can change', 'give choices more clearly' and 'try different approaches in my work'.

Sarah went on to ensure that this training became embedded in the school training programme. She was determined to continue to share her knowledge and understanding of autism with colleagues to support their journey towards the autism friendly workplace.

Sarah concluded: 'I believe that it is crucial to involve staff in training and in the practice of self-reflection. I believe that my intervention was relevant to improving practice and I hope it will prove beneficial for our residential students. I hope my involvement in the training group can support others to use the "autism lens" more widely in practice.'

Conclusion

At the time of writing, Sarah's co-workers were still experimenting with these new ideas so it was not possible for her to gather evidence of their impact on practice. Nonetheless, this small-scale case study exemplifies the considerable potential of workplace auditing and action planning, and illustrates how practitioners can make a difference to the quality of the autism friendly workplace by positively and constructively sharing knowledge and expertise with peers. Simple, well-focused questionnaires and informal discussions allowed Sarah to draw her co-workers' attention to a widespread weakness in current provision highlighted by the audit, examine it in detail via critical self-reflection, and then explore the knowledge and skills that might help them to address the problem. If each of her 12 colleagues succeeded in reducing prompt-dependency in the light of this training, there is no doubt that there would be considerable benefits for their students with autism.

In Sarah's case study the co-workers were lucky enough to be able to proceed with their transformation of practice within an ethos of trust and care for staff as well as students, with the luxury of time allocated specifically to professional development, and with the ongoing support of Sarah and other colleagues. However, change is not always accommodated in these helpful ways.

In the final chapter of this book we will look at some of the barriers to change that can, and all too frequently do, undermine workplace improvement, by critically examining the concept of the 'implementation gap'. We will define the meaning of this concept, examine its implications, and explore why it needs to be better, and more widely, understood if national strategies for autism are to make any real and lasting difference to the lives of people with autism.

References

AET (Autism Education Trust) (2011) *What is Good Practice in Autism Education?* London: National Autistic Society.

Batten, A. & Daly, J. (2006) *Make School Make Sense: Autism and Education in Scotland – The Reality for Families*, London: National Autistic Society.

Billstedt, E.I., Gillberg, C. & Gillberg, C. (2011) Aspects of quality of life in adults diagnosed with autism in childhood: a population-based study, *Autism* 15/7, 8–21.

DfCMS (2010) The Equality Act. Accessible: https://www.gov.uk/equality-act-2010-guidance (accessed Feb. 2014).

DfES (Department for Education and Skills) (2002) *Autistic Spectrum Disorders: Good Practice Guidance*, Nottingham: DfES Publications.

Department of Health (DoH) (2010) *Fulfilling & Rewarding Lives: The Strategy for Adults with Autism in England.* Accessible: http://webarchive.nationalarchives. gov.uk/20130107105354/http://www.dh.gov.uk/prod_consum_dh/groups/dh_ digitalassets/@dh/@en/@ps/documents/digitalasset/dh_113405.pdf   (accessed Feb. 2014).

LCD (Leonard Cheshire Disability) (2013) *Ending 1-minute Care.* Accessible: www. lcdisability.org (accessed Feb. 2014).

MacKay, T.A.W.N. & Dunlop, A.W.A. (2004) *The Development of a National Training Framework for Autistic Spectrum Disorders: A Study of Training for Professionals Working in the Field of ASD in Scotland*, Glasgow: National Autistic Society and University of Strathclyde.

National Autistic Society (undated) *Autism Accreditation Programme.* Accessible: http:// www.autism.org.uk/our-services/autism-accreditation.aspx (accessed Feb. 2014).

NCS (National Care Standards) (undated) *National Care Standards: School Care Accommodation Services.* Accessible: http://www.nationalcarestandards.org/ (accessed Feb. 2014).

NHS Health Scotland (2011) Appendix 5: Equality and human rights legislative requirements, in *Health Inequalities Impact Assessment*, Edinburgh: NHS Health Scotland. Accessible: http://www.healthscotland.com/equalities/equalityact.aspx (accessed April 2013).

NIASA (National Initiative for Autism: Screening and Assessment) (2003) *National Autism Plan for Children*, London: National Autistic Society.

ORO (Open Research Online) (2003) *Distributed Leadership: A Review of the Literature*: Accessible: http://oro.open.ac.uk/8534/1/ (accessed Feb. 2014).

Ravet, J. (2012) From interprofessional education to interprofessional practice: exploring the implementation gap, *Professional Development in Education*, 38/1, 49–64.

Scottish Government (2008) *Commissioning Services for People on the Autism Spectrum*, Edinburgh: Scottish Government.

Scottish Government (2011) *The Scottish Strategy for Autism.* Accessible: http:// www.scotland.gov.uk/Resource/Doc/361926/0122373.pdf (accessed Feb. 2014).

SIGN (Scottish Intercollegiate Guidelines Network) (2007) *Assessment, Diagnosis and Clinical Interventions for Children and Young People with Autism Spectrum Disorders: A National Clinical Guideline.* Accessible: http://www.sign.ac.uk/ pdf/sign98.pdf (accessed Feb. 2014).

Timperley, H.S. (2005) Distributed leadership: developing theory from practice, *Journal of Curriculum Studies*, 37/4, 395–420.

Villa, R.A. & Thousand, J.S. (eds) (2005) *Creating an Inclusive School* (2nd edition), Virginia (USA): ASCD.

Chapter 7

Supporting change

Bridging the implementation gap

There must be many practitioners who attend professional development courses in autism and then return to the workplace brimming with enthusiasm for new ideas, itching to have a go. Like Sarah in chapter 6, they might undertake a workplace audit, collaboratively identify priority targets and then plan for implementation, hoping to cascade good practice and initiate positive change. This process can lead to significant improvements in professional practice which, in the best-case scenario, generates wider workplace improvement and positive outcomes for clients. A range of theory, practice and research has been presented in this book to explore and substantiate this claim.

However, not infrequently, one's enthusiasm for new ideas is quickly tempered by the harsh realities of the workplace. For various reasons, new initiatives can be squashed before they even get off the ground, draining practitioners of motivation and energy, and ensuring, by default, the continuation of the status quo. Professionals, in this scenario, have come up against the 'implementation gap' (Supovitz & Weinbaum 2008) – the difficulty of bridging the gap between theory and practice.

The problem of the implementation gap is rarely discussed or even alluded to in autism research, and yet it is a ubiquitous issue wherever change is afoot across education, health and social care services (Villa & Thousand 2005, Fauth & Mahdon 2007, Drahota et al. 2012). It is the 'elephant in the room' that can quietly undermine the spread of good practice envisioned in workplace development plans as well as regional and national autism strategies. It is therefore a force that needs to be anticipated, understood and taken into consideration at every strategic level.

In the final chapter of this book we will explore the concept of the implementation gap by first considering a case study. We will then critically discuss the barriers to implementation that the case study identifies, the implications of these barriers and how they might be addressed. The aim is to achieve a realistic assessment of the potential for change in workplace settings, and a practical approach to maximising this potential.

The implementation gap: what is it?

The notion of the implemention gap is defined as 'the problematic issue of the translation from prescribed policy to enacted practice' (Supovitz & Weinbaum 2008 p. 25). We experience the implementation gap when, despite our enthusiasm and hard work aimed at introducing new workplace practices, uptake fails to gain real momentum. We all know when we have hit the implementation gap because we feel frustrated by its effects, though we may not be able to put our finger on exactly where things went wrong. If we could find out, it would enable us to identify the factors within the workplace that facilitate successful implementation, as well as pinpointing the factors that delay or inhibit the process of change. An understanding of these factors can then inform our next steps. Analysis of the implementation gap is therefore important for those interested in enhancing service provision for people with autism.

So far in this book we have explored a range of factors that can undermine the transfer of theory into practice. These include:

• myths and misunderstandings that distort perceptions of autism
• complications arising from ongoing shifts and inconsistencies within the autism research
• conflicting inclusion discourses and associated practice dilemmas
• weaknesses in the assessment and individualisation process
• the difficulty of establishing 'what works' with regard to autism strategies and interventions
• difficulties defining and analysing challenging behaviour and determining environmental/internal triggers
• challenges linked to joint training and interprofessional practice
• poor strategic planning and leadership for the autism friendly workplace

This list reflects some of the complications associated with autism theory and practice and the considerable challenge of implementation across autism services. Nonetheless, these factors are, largely, related to the continuing evolution of autism research and the effective use of the autism lens. The latter, arguably, can be addressed via good autism training. This argument has been made again and again across this book.

However, as we shall see, not all barriers to implementation can be resolved via research and training. Here, I am referring to structural and cultural barriers associated with particular service contexts and specific workplace settings. These barriers lie beyond the reach and influence of autism trainers and autism training. What are they?

Case study: factors inhibiting the implementation of good autism practice

In a small-scale case study already outlined in chapter 5, we explored the development of interprofessional practice amongst a group of ten students supporting clients with autism in education, health and social care, who undertook a postgraduate Certificate in Autism and Learning in a higher education establishment. The perceptions of their line managers and funders were also explored (see Ravet 2012 for further details).

Here, we will consider the findings of the wider study into the efficacy and impact of advanced interprofessional education in autism and its implications for professional development across autism services. These findings are summarised in table 7.1.

Table 7.1 An evaluative case study of IPE in Autism and Learning: outcomes relating to professional development in Autism and Learning

Changes in attitude and perception	*Facilitating factors:* • Increased confidence in practice • Greater willingness to be pro-active, initiate change and show leadership *'The programme made me go and find out more about legislation and education policies…and now I can spout this forth when I'm fighting for issues.'* *Inhibiting factors:* • Negative attitude to autism amongst colleagues • Resistance to change amongst colleagues • Powerlessness to address these problems linked to low status *'I do think that there is a lack of guidance about responsibilities for pupils on the spectrum and some of my colleagues are not interested in learning about autism or taking responsibility for pupils with the condition in their care.'*
Acquisition of knowledge and skills	*Facilitating factors:* • Improved and updated knowledge and understanding of autism and learning • Improved and updated knowledge and understanding of policy, legislation, literature and research relating to autism and learning

Table 7.1 Continued

| | • Greater knowledge and understanding of strategies and interventions and their evidence base
• Enhanced capacity for critical reflection upon practice

'The course has given me more confidence to use the knowledge I had as well as expanding upon this. Topics of each assignment directed me towards literature which I was previously unaware of, which increased my understanding of ASD, enabling me to understand more about the child I work with.'

Inhibiting factors:
• Gaps in course regarding specific service approaches and provision

'Some more emphasis on lower-functioning children with ASD and a shift away from the traditional curriculum to daily life skills would have been useful to non-teaching staff.' |
| **Behavioural changes** | **Facilitating factors:**
• Improved workplace practice (e.g. use of ABA charts to analyse behaviour, use of person-centred planning to enhance participation, better target-setting)
• More effective support for and collaboration with parents and colleagues
• More active on working groups and in out-reach
• More likely to apply for promotion

'My handling of what I deemed to be 'misbehaviour' on the part of my pupils is now very different.'

Inhibiting factors:
• Lack of time for interprofessional collaboration (education contexts only)
• Lack of funding for wider staff IPE (education contexts only)

'I found working collaboratively with outside agencies a challenge in terms of being able to organise time to have a professional dialogue and to meet.' |

Changes in organisational practice

Facilitating factors:
• Working towards better autism provision and enhanced inclusion across the workplace
• Working towards wider staff training

'The person-centred planning approach that was picked up on the course – this has had a huge influence on our review meetings. We are using that a lot more across the school, not just with autistic children but with all children with special needs.'

Inhibiting factors:
• Structures and working practices inflexible (especially in education sector)
• Lack of time/resources
• Policy clashes (e.g. curriculum policy v. inclusion policy)
• Lack of leadership
• Limited dissemination of national guidance

'The main barrier for me at the moment is time...it's very difficult to sit down and evaluate what I am doing on a regular basis. That would be something I would like to do, regularly review what we are doing.'

Perceived benefits to service users

• Enhanced inclusion for clients with autism
• Needs met more efficiently and effectively via higher-quality support and intervention
• Greater consistency of support within and across services
• More opportunities for client participation
• Improved client learning/well-being

'I feel that there will be a great benefit to the child in my setting as I can directly support them...as a result of the new knowledge and understanding ... Also, through educating the wider staff, children will also benefit from the positive ethos.'

Inhibiting factors:
• Tokenism

'(A barrier is) the school paying lip-service and ticking boxes without full commitment.'

Discussion

It is clear from the findings above that the students on the IPE programme had undergone a transformation in their knowledge and understanding of autism that enabled them to enhance their skills and improve their own professional practice, wider workplace practice and outcomes for their clients with autism. Their line managers and funders provided further evidence for these claims (see Ravet 2011, Ravet 2012). However, it also clear that, despite their best efforts, many of the students who attended the programme returned to their workplaces only to be confronted with a wide range of barriers, beyond their control, that inhibited the uptake of good autism practice. The key purpose of this chapter is to explore and analyse these barriers, so we shall turn to them now and then discuss their implications.

Negative attitudes and resistance to change

Negative attitudes towards the inclusion of individuals with autism, and resistance to new autism practices, were recurring problems for some practitioners in the case study. This was reported most frequently amongst those from the education sector. Unfortunately, such attitudes in schools are widely reported in the autism research, as discussed in chapter 2 (Humphrey & Lewis 2008, Jones et al. 2008). However, the problem with such resistance is that it may not simply be linked, in a straightforward way, to lack of understanding of autism. Rather, resistance can be highly 'overdetermined' – that is to say it may be triggered by a range of underlying personal dispositions and emotions such as fear of the unknown or fear of loss of status and power (Fauth & Mahdon 2007). Such underlying fears are not likely to be diminished by autism training alone, but require organisations to take positive steps to address anxiety and minimise resistance in the face of change.

Research indicates that this is a complex matter in any service setting (Erwin & Garmen (2010). However, Goltz and Hietapelto (2002) (in Fauth & Mahdon 2007) suggest that it can be approached by creating an ethos of support, transparency, safety and open communication in the workplace, in which fears are shared and resistance explored, rather than simply being ignored, dismissed or even suppressed. Fauth and Mahdon (2007), researching in a health and social care setting, acknowledge that 'resistors usually have a valid message' (p. 51). Thus, ideally, all staff should contribute to the change process, and managers should listen carefully to concerns and seek joint solutions that instil confidence and promote openness and acceptance of new ideas.

There is a growing awareness of the vital influence of practitioner attitudes when introducing new interventions in the workplace (NICE 2007).

However, this is, perhaps, less well embedded in educational settings (Villa & Thousand 2005).

Time

Another recurring inhibiting factor across the case study findings was the lack of time to put new autism initiatives into practice alongside daily business in the workplace. Time is a perennial and complex problem for many practitioners and is associated with heavy workloads and the widespread intensification of life at the chalk-face (Cheung et al. 2013, Kasari & Smith 2013). The problem is also linked to structural barriers such as workload policies and timetabling issues (McCartney 2006) and to the policy context where time for autism initiatives competes with a range of other equally pressing policy demands. Clearly, this combination of tensions can create considerable stress for practitioners – all the more so because they lack the power to control them.

The issue of time and how it constrains professional development and practice is likely to be a ubiquitous service issue. It can only be addressed by service managers who are willing to evaluate workloads and review priorities to ensure that time is made available for good autism practice to take hold and thrive. This challenge is not optional if we are serious about supporting change in autism services, yet the problem can seem intractable. However, Villa and Thousand (2005) suggest a number of 'strategies for expanding time' (p. 66) based on their own research into the change process in schools. These are summarised in table. 7.2. Though these ideas are simple, they may make the difference between workplace change and workplace stagnation. However, more research is required to establish an evidence base for their efficacy.

Table. 7.2 Strategies for expanding time (Villa & Thousand 2005)

- **Borrow time**: re-arrange things so that time is taken here, and added there, to create a specific space for discussion of new autism initiatives
- **Release time**: make a joint decision to transfer the use of an existing time slot over to autism development
- **Schedule time**: build regular interprofessional meetings into the timetable
- **Free-up time**: organise more joint working so that certain individual members of staff can be released by peers to work on autism development planning
- **Purchase time**: hire temporary staff to replace permanent staff to create time for development or training, or pay staff to work on a Saturday morning or bank holiday
- **Found time**: use 'snow days' and other unexpected times for planning and discussion
- **New time**: incentivise staff to rationalise their work to create regular pockets of time for new initiatives.

Policy clashes

Government policies can sometimes be a problem, as well as a solution, for practitioners supporting clients with autism. For example, some of the students in the case study worked in contexts where there was no clear consensus about the meaning of inclusion policy and how it should be enacted. This meant that practitioners were responding differently and inconsistently to client needs, creating tensions amongst staff and between staff and management, and doubtless generating difficulties for the clients involved. This issue was discussed in detail in chapter 2.

The wide range of government policies that impact on workplace settings may also clash in practice so that the demands of one somehow conflict with the demands of another. The example highlighted in the case study is the clash between curriculum policy in Scottish schools, which emphasises learning through group work and cross-curricular themes, and inclusion policy, which requires teachers to meet the needs of children with autism who may find group work challenging and find it difficult to make links across subject boundaries. How are teachers to resolve such conflicts? Unfortunately, there is no easy answer to this question. It can only be addressed and resolved through open and informed debate in the workplace, aimed at establishing a shared understanding.

Funding and resourcing

Autism interventions are often labour intensive, especially in their initial stages, as they require practitioners to learn about the condition and draw on new and often unfamiliar approaches and protcols. They may therefore call for additional staff training in autism, additional human resources such as assistants and advocates, and extra space for quiet, one-to-one support away from busy or over-stimulating contexts. All of these come at a considerable premium in the workplace. Access to funding to provide these resources was therefore an area for improvement highlighted in the case study findings, and clearly requires attention at government, national and local service level.

Some funding officers who contributed to this study indicated that improvements in autism services were local priorities and would be funded wherever possible. However, others expressed confusion over priorities in the face of competing policy agendas. This problem is highlighted in the wider research (Batten & Daly 2006). Clarification of funding priorities at all levels is therefore vital if the rhetoric of inclusive autism provision is to become a reality. Though considerable sums have been made available as a result of national strategies in the UK, questions remain as to how this funding will be distributed, who decides and whether it will be ring fenced to ensure that it is used to the benefit of people with autism. Evaluation of impact is also a key issue if we are to ensure best value for money. Funding is therefore a lynchpin of service improvement, but it may be difficult to secure and necessitate choices amongst competing priorities – especially during times of economic contraction. The UK national autism strategies may help in this respect by ensuring that improvement across autism services is at the top of service agendas. However, this remains to be seen.

Conclusions and implications

The case study above provides examples of the implementation gap as it relates to autism practice in a particular geographical location within ten specific workplace contexts. Though it is inappropriate to draw generalisations from this small-scale qualitative study, the findings replicate those of similar evaluative studies (e.g. Tait & Dunlop 2005) and are likely to resonate with autism practitioners across education, health and social care settings.

What is striking about the barriers to implementation discussed is that they do not imply either limitations in practitioner knowledge, understanding or skill, nor weaknesses in training provision. Rather, they are constraints within the workplace itself, which practitioners and educators cannot possibly influence, yet they are highly resilient hurdles which, if ignored, can operate like a black hole swallowing up good intentions and worthy training initiatives.

Clearly, for autism services to improve, implementation has to be successful and sustained. A key issue is therefore whether it is possible to predict exactly where new initiatives might 'stick' or 'slip' following implementation (Supovitz & Weinbaum 2008). This issue is still not well understood, but in their study of the implementation gap in the education sector, Supovitz and Weinbaum (2008) found that operationalising good practice is rarely a straightforward, unidirectional process, but is, in fact, a process of 'iterative refraction' (ibid. p. 151) in which new initiatives must be repeatedly adjusted and adapted as they are brought into practice in the workplace. This continuous adjustment is necessary to compensate for and/ or accommodate the barriers outlined above and to enable implementation to progress. It follows that where there is a failure to identify barriers and to make appropriate adjustments, service improvement will be seriously undermined or fail.

This implies that a collaborative approach to autism service improvement, involving policy makers, autism educators and researchers, service managers and practitioners at local service level, is essential in order to maximise the benefits of training and the potential for service improvement. The need for such partnerships is already being explored in the emerging field of 'implementation science' (Drahota et al. 2012, Kelly and Perkins 2012), which is concerned with how to make medical, psychological, social and educational interventions effective in different real-life contexts. Implementation science proceeds from the assumption that the success of implementation cannot be taken for granted, but is inextricably linked to social context such as staff and organisational preparedness and management readiness for implementation and change (ibid.).

The use of implementation science is fairly well established in the field of health research but is relatively new to autism research (Kasari & Smith 2013). According to Dingfelder and Mandell (2011) this is problematic since 'there is growing evidence that efficacious interventions for autism are rarely adopted or successfully implemented in public mental health and education systems' (p. 597). They link this to the poor fit between 'the interventions and the needs and capacities of the setting', which prevents new approaches and strategies from progressing from 'implementation to institutionalisation' (ibid.). This means that individuals with autism cannot benefit from them and represents a significant crisis for the autism community.

Various models have been developed to support the adaptation of interventions to the practice context and the practice context to the intervention within community health contexts (e.g. Glisson & Schoenwald 2005). Such models apply a collaborative, community-based approach in which stakeholders' perceptions are taken into account, and in which participatory planning and decision-making are key to fostering ownership and acceptance. However, these models do not have a direct bearing on autism interventions and implementation, though the ideas are transferrable. This is slowly beginning to happen.

For example, Drahota et al. (2012) are currently formulating an 'autism model of implementation' that will be specifically designed to enhance the implementation of good autism practice amongst community agencies in the US. The model is being developed collaboratively between academia and community stakeholders in order to tailor it to the needs of the local autism community and to the realities of the workplace. It is therefore 'contextually specific' and will take account of the unique organisational and individual service factors that influence the implementation process within the community-based settings under consideration (ibid.). Initial studies indicate that these factors include training, attitudes to change, attitudes to evidence-based practice, funding, time, resources, motivation, skills and capacity (ibid.) – a list that clearly mirrors the factors that emerged in the study above. The developmental work associated with Drahota et al.'s study is still being researched, so the model is yet to be fully articulated, piloted and refined. However, it is suggestive of the way forward for the development of autism services and indicative of the degree of collaborative working and joint analysis required, at local service level, to ensure effective and sustained service improvement.

Arguably, more implementation science is required in the field of autism in order to bridge the implementation gap between research and practice.

This would generate an evidence base for effectiveness and impact in autism services and help us to identify and better understand the barriers to improvement within different service contexts. Arguably, this is the key to ensuring that individuals with autism benefit as fully as possible and have the services they deserve.

Where do we go from here?

In the introduction to this book I claimed that its purpose was to shine a light on professional action and impact across autism services in the context of the Autism Act (2009 (England), 2011 (Northern Ireland)) and the national autism strategies in Scotland and Wales (Scottish Government 2011, Welsh Assembly Government 2008). The focus on professional action concerns what we actually do to bring about positive change to enhance accessibility, inclusion and participation for people with autism. I hope that the research-based critique of the current state of our knowledge and understanding of the condition, the strategies for supporting inclusion and participation and for working interprofessionally to achieve autism friendly services, will contribute to our current understanding of what such professional action entails, and the considerable challenge it poses. The role of education and training in achieving high-quality professionalism in autism cannot be underestimated.

The focus on 'impact' is of equal importance to ensure that professional action is well targeted and effective in maximising successful outcomes for clients with autism. I hope that readers have by now grasped the complex interplay of factors, associated with the implementation gap, that can have a bearing on impact, and their decisive influence on progress and change across autism services. This complexity must be more fully acknowledged by policy makers and service providers, for we cannot hope to transform the landscape of service provision for people with autism without effective integration of policy, research and practice and a well-planned, research-based approach to the evaluation of implementation. This will depend, in no small measure, on exploring the relevance of implementation science to service development in autism. Ultimately, however, it is practitioners who will make implementation succeed. It is dedicated and well-informed professional action that will transform the lives of people with autism.

References

Autism Act (2009) London: The Stationery Office. Accessible: http://www.legislation. gov.uk/ukpga/2009/15/pdfs/ukpga_20090015_en.pdf (accessed July 2014).

Autism Act (Northern Ireland) (2011) London: The Stationery Office.

Batten, A. & Daly, J. (2006) *Make School Make Sense: Autism and Education in Scotland – The Reality for Families*, London: National Autistic Society. Accessible: bera.ac.uk/publications (accessed May 2008).

Cheung, G., Tremblath, D., Areiuli, J. & Togher, L. (2013) The impact of workplace factors on evidence-based speech & language pathology practice for children with ASD, *International Journal of Speech and Language Pathology*, 15/4, 396–406.

Dingfelder, H.E. & Mandell, D.S. (2011) Bridging the research-to-practice gap in autism intervention: an application of diffusion of innovation theory, *Journal of Autism and Developmental Disorders*, 41/5, 597–609.

Drahota, A., Aarons, G.K. & Stahmer, A.C. (2012) Developing the autism model of implementation for autism spectrum disorder community providers: study protocol, *Implementation Science*, 7/85, 1–10.

Erwin, D.G. & Garman, A.N. (2010) Resistance to organisational change: linking research & practice, *Leadership and Organisation Development Journal*, 31/1, 39–56.

Fauth, R. & Mahdon, M. (2007) *Improving Social & Health Care Services: People Management Knowledge Review 16*, London: Social Care Institute for Excellence (SCIE).

Glisson, C. & Schoenwald, S.K. (2005) The ARC organisational and community intervention strategy for implementing evidence-based children's mental health treatments, *Mental Health Services Research*, 7/4, 243–259.

Goltz, S.M. & Hietapelto, A. (2002) 'Using the operant and strategic contingencies models of power to understand resistance to change', *Journal of Organizational Behaviour Management*, 22/3, 3–22.

HMIE (2006) *Education for Pupils with Autism Spectrum Disorders*, Livingston: HMIE.

Humphrey, N. & Lewis, S. (2008) What does 'inclusion' mean for pupils on the autistic spectrum in mainstream secondary schools? *Journal of Research in Special Educational Needs*, 8/3, 132–140.

Jones, G., English, A., Guldberg, K., Jordan, R., Richardson, P. & Waltz, M. (2008) *Educational Provision for Children & Young People on the Autism Spectrum Living in England: A Review of Current Practice, Issues and Challenges*, London: Autism Education Trust. Accessible: www.autismeducationtrust.org. uk (accessed Nov. 2008).

Kasari, C. & Smith, T. (2013) Interventions in schools for children with ASD: methods and recommendations, *Autism*, 17/3, 254–267.

Kelly, B. & Perkins, D.F. (2012) *Handbook of Implementation Science for Psychology in Education*, Cambridge: Cambridge University Press.

McCartney, E. (2006) Interprofessional & interagency working (Paper 14), *The Research & Policy Discourses of Service Integration: ESRC Seminar 1 Proceedings*, Aberdeen: University of Aberdeen.

NICE (National Institute for Health & Clinical Excellence) (2007) How to change practice. Accessible: http://www.nice.org.uk/media/D33/8D/Howtochangepractice1. pdf (accessed April 2014).

Ravet, J. (2011) Interprofessional training in autism: impact on professional development and workplace practice, *Good Autism Practice*, 12/1, 79–87.

Ravet, J. (2012) From interprofessional education to interprofessional practice: exploring the implementation gap, *Professional Development in Education*, 38/1, 49–64.

Scottish Government (2011) *The Scottish Strategy for Autism: Overview*, Edinburgh: Scottish Government.

Supovitz, J.A. (2008) Implementation as iterative refraction, in J.A. Supovitz & E.H. Weinbaum (eds), *The Implementation Gap: Understanding Reform in High Schools*, New York: Teachers College Press.

Supovitz, J.A. & Weinbaum, E.H. (eds) (2008) *The Implementation Gap: Understanding Reform in High Schools*, New York: Teachers College Press.

Tait, C. & Dunlop, A.W.A. (2005) *The Impact of Training on Practice: Insights from Postgraduate Study of Autism*. ISEC Conference 2005, Glasgow.

Villa, R.A. & Thousand, J.S. (2005) *Creating an Inclusive School* (2nd edition), Virginia USA: Association for Supervision and Curriculum Development (ASCD).

Welsh Assembly Government (2008) *Autism Spectrum Disorder Strategic Action Plan for Wales*, Cardiff: Welsh Assembly Government.

Index